BAD NEWS

BAD NEWS

The Best of Esquire Magazine's Dubious Achievements, 1961–1984

By the editors of Esquire

Designed by Muney Rivers

AN ESQUIRE PRESS BOOK
AVON
PUBLISHERS OF BARD, CAMELOT, DISCUS AND FLARE BOOKS

BAD NEWS: THE BEST OF ESQUIRE MAGAZINE'S DUBIOUS
ACHIEVEMENTS, 1961–1984 is an original publication of Esquire Press/Avon
Books. This work has never before appeared in book form.

Material in this book has previously appeared in *Esquire*.

AVON BOOKS
A division of
The Hearst Corporation
1790 Broadway
New York, New York 10019

Library of Congress Cataloging in Publication Data

Bad news.
1. Curiosities and wonders.   I. Esquire (New York, N.Y.)
AG243.B25 1984   032'.02   83-17238
ISBN 0-380-85712-X

First Avon Printing, January 1984

"Men are mad."

—Twiggy

CONTENTS

✶ INTRODUCTION ✶

You're holding in your hands final and absolute proof that civilization moves forward by inches and sometimes slips on a banana peel.

Bad News is a collection of the best Dubious Achievements selected by *Esquire* since the publication of its first annual Dubious Achievement Awards in January 1962. As such, it is history—a review of some of the silliest events, dumbest quotes, and most misguided behavior of recent times. It should also be a learning tool: if we don't learn from the mistakes of the past, we are doomed to repeat them.

Esquire's Dubious Achievement Awards remain one of the magazine's best-known and best-selling features. All year long, the editors clip newspapers, collect photographs, and jot notes on happenings in the world that are so dubious as to be laughable. Toward the end of the year, the items and photos are reviewed and a hundred or so finalists are selected. These include nominations for the worst movie of the year, the rainiest day of the year, fun couples, and dubiously behaved celebrities, as well as reports on bloopers and goofs from every corner of life. Then, after each of the items is verified, the Awards are published in the January issue.

So, you see, the editors of *Esquire* don't make up the bad news, we just report it. Relentlessly.

WRETCHED EXCESS

KHOMEINI TIMES MUST A MAN TURN HIS HEAD?

1979 King Khalid of Saudi Arabia ordered a special navigation system for his private 747. The system was designed to point his throne toward Mecca—no matter which direction the plane was flying in.

NOW ALL HE NEEDS IS TWO TIN CANS AND HE CAN TALK TO BULGARIA

1971 Francis Johnson, a retired carpenter from Darwin, Minnesota, saved string for twenty-one years, ending up with a five-ton, eleven-foot-high ball of twine.

*

AND A WALLET LIFE OF THIRTY

1976 According to a government report, A.I.D. shipped to Thailand a 139-year supply of condoms, which have a shelf life of 5 to 10 years.

*

BUT NO ANCHOVIES, THANK GOD

1983 Waste from a frozen-pizza plant clogged the industrial sewage system of Wellston, Ohio, with approximately 400,000 gallons of sludge made up of flour, tomato paste, cheese, vegetables, and pepperoni. Engineering companies employed by the city said a $500,000 conveyor system was needed to dry and decompose the sludge so it could be safely buried.

*

AND IT SHALL BE MY DUTY NOT ONLY TO PROSECUTE TO THE LIMIT OF THE LAW ALL PERSONS ACCUSED OF CRIMES PERPETRATED WITHIN THIS COUNTY BUT TO DEFEND WITH EQUAL VIGOR THE RIGHTS AND PRIVILEGES OF ALL ITS CITIZENS

1975 To avoid being guilty of sex discrimination, Baltimore County Liquor Board chairman Joseph Hess ordered a male nightclub go-go dancer to wear "a bra or something to conceal the entire nipple area and lower breast."

LAST GAS BEFORE EXIT

1979 Trinity Church, the three-hundred-year-old Episcopal parish in New York, ran an ad entitled "Death and the Gasoline Shortage" to help sell resting places in its new 5,100-space high-rise mausoleum. According to the ad, by "purchasing now, you will save your family money and gas" because the mausoleum was "reachable by public transportation."

*

TIRED OF THE SAME OLD LOBSTER THERMIDOR?

1975 A company in Miami introduced Snif-T-Panties, women's underwear scented with a variety of fragrances. Among the scents offered: banana, rose, popcorn, whiskey, pickle, and pizza.

*

Funny, She Doesn't Look Jewish

1982 Four hundred pets in Hewlett, Long Island, were invited to a "bark mitzvah" for a thirteen-year-old female mutt named Greggie "Lump Lump" Taylor.

6

FUNNY THING IS, HIS VILLAGE SCENES ARE SO REALISTIC YOU'D SWEAR THEY WERE PHOTOGRAPHS
1980 A man at the University of Southern California was accused of assault after surreptitiously painting the toenails of dozens of women. The man would sit next to women and drop things on the floor. Each time he bent down to pick up an object, he would paint another toenail.

✳

HOW COME YOU NEVER HEAR ABOUT THE 98 PERCENT THAT ARE A CREDIT TO THEIR RACE?
1975 After breaking into an illegal still in West Bengal, India, and drinking the moonshine liquor, a herd of 150 drunken elephants demolished seven concrete buildings and trampled twenty huts, killing five people and injuring twelve others.

✳

STANLEY KOWALSKI FOR MURJANI
1980 Danya Pakilla of Montclair, New Jersey, began marketing T-shirts with wet-looking sweat marks under the arms.

✳

SNOT FUNNY
1981 *The New York Times* reported that thousands of Americans are addicted to nasal spray.

✳

A TASTE OF MONEY

1982 Charging forty cents for a twelve-tablet pack, a Danish company introduced Stimorol— "chewing gum for the rich."

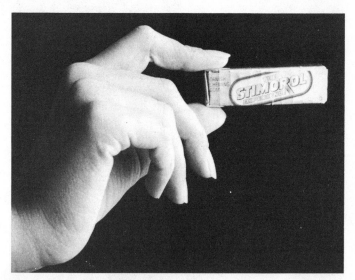

The Clifford Irving Gold Pen-and-Pencil Set for Journalistic Integrity to:

Janet Cooke, of *The Washington Post*, who was forced to return the 1981 Pulitzer Prize she won for a profile of an eight-year-old heroin addict who never existed.

And Accepting for Miss Cooke...

A student in Richard Astle's San Diego State creative writing class turned in a story called "Anthony's World." Except for a change of name, age, and home town, it was plagiarized word for word from Janet Cooke's *Washington Post* article "Jimmy's World."

Youth-Oriented Music Ensemble Exhibits
Displeasure at Commonplace Brown Confection

1980 Van Halen, a heavy-metal rock quartet, required that two pounds of M&M candies be provided backstage at their concerts but that all the brown-colored M&Ms be removed. When one promoter at a midwestern college forgot to extract the brown candies, Van Halen trashed the dressing room and stage.

Louder, Louder, Oh, My God, Louder!

1981 New York inventor David Lloyd came out with "rock and roll pants" for men and women, bikinis that hook up to a stereo and cause vibrations in the crotch.

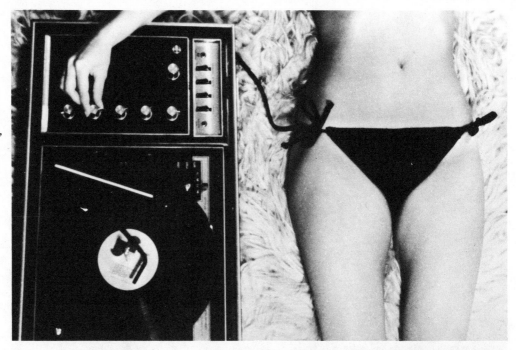

WAKE UP, BETTY BOB, IT'S TIME FOR MASTERPIECE THEATRE

1981 Bert, Fred, and Ralph Jett, three brothers in Kanawha County, West Virginia, had a $7,800 dish antenna constructed in their yard to improve their TV reception.

Why Didn't They Just Invite Lawrence Welk?

1981 To highlight a culinary fair in Peekskill, New York, architect Seymour Arkaway and chef Franz Eichenauer constructed a giant cornball.

Meanwhile Down on the Bowery, Rin Tin Tin Is Grubbing Butts and Washing Windshields

1978 While in New York for an engagement at Radio City Music Hall, Lassie stayed in a $380-a-day suite at the Plaza hotel.

Proof That If God Isn't Dead He Maybe Wishes He Were

1968 The dean, a canon, and three cathedral officials parachuted off St. Paul's Cathedral in London to attract British youth to religion.

TSRIF ACIREMA EES

1976 Plennie Wingo walked backward from San Francisco to Santa Maria, California, wearing glasses with rearview mirrors.

HOLD THE TOMATOES

1981 Twenty-six members of the Delta Tau Delta fraternity at the University of Illinois's Champaign-Urbana campus were evicted from their house after several of them decided to "get naked" at a party, piled on top of a co-ed, and yelled, "Sex sandwich! Sex sandwich!"

✳

OFFICER, ARREST THAT GROUNDHOG!

1972 The District of Columbia Court of Appeals ruled that police have a right to break into a pay toilet if they see two pairs of legs under the door.

✳

WORST NEW FLAVOR

1980 Researchers at Cornell University reported that they were able to make wine out of cheese whey.

✳

HOT DAMN! LET'S DROP IT ON CHINA

1975 Midas's Last Touch Metalworks of Los Angeles came out with a $25,000, 18-karat-gold phallus. It was nine and one half inches long and two inches in diameter, and weighed over five pounds.

✳

HE DID IT HIS WAY

1979 President Francisco Macías Nguema of Equatorial Guinea was overthrown after eleven years in office. In that time, he murdered ten of his original twelve cabinet ministers, buried thirty-six enemies up to their necks to be eaten alive by insects, and hanged another group in public while loudspeakers blared a rendition of "Those Were the Days."

✳

13

**WE'RE SIXTY
RUSSKI BIRDIES
WE'D LIKE YOU
ALL TO KNOW
WE DOO-DOO AND
WE DOO-WAH
WE HOPE YOU
LIKE OUR SHOW**

1976 Soviet machine fitter Leonid Germatski reportedly trained a choir of sixty songbirds to sing Russian folk songs and Strauss waltzes. According to Tass, the bird choir, led by a blackbird and a nightingale, surpassed even ice hockey in popularity among Soviet TV viewers.

*

...That Works Out to About a Million and a Half Dollars a Month

1969 According to the Boston *Record American,* Jackie and Aristotle Onassis spent somewhere between $15 million and $20 million on various domestic items, such as houses (nine of those), art, jewelry, etc., in the first year of their marriage.

IT'S YOU, MOHAMMED S. A. AL FASSI! IT'S REALLY YOU!

1978 Saudi Arabian sheikh Mohammed S. A. al Fassi bought a mansion in Beverly Hills for $2.4 million and then spent an additional $2.5 million redecorating. The house was painted lime green. The detail on a dozen flesh-toned human statues included pubic hair, and a row of Romanesque urns containing plastic flowers was set around the estate.

14

FOR ZEE SPECIAL TONIGHT, WE HAVE DERRIÈRE DE BOEUF À LA FILBERT...

1977 Filbert Maestas of Denver was convicted of breaking into a warehouse and stealing meat. He later learned he had taken 1,200 beef rectums.

...AND ZERE EES TO FOLLOW A SUPERB VACHE DE MER AU KLUTZ...

When four severed cow's heads washed up on East Hampton, New York, beaches, a spokesman for the state environmental-conservation department said whoever was responsible was "somewhere between a klutz and a jerk." The culprit turned out to be *New York Times* food writer Craig Claiborne, who had bought the heads for a tête de veau vinaigrette recipe. He found the heads nearly impossible to skin and so tossed the remains into the sea.

...ET POUR LE DESSERT, WE HAVE TARTE DE SOIXANTE- NEUF À LA LUNDY AVEC CRÈME FRAÎCHE. MAGNIFIQUE!

Don Lundy, a Dallas baker, created pastries in sixty-three different male and female sexual designs and called them porno cakes.

✳

PROMISE THEM ANYTHING, BUT GIVE THEM CHIQUITA NUMBER 5

1976 To mask the smell of sewage, the Concord Light and Power Commission of Cabarrus County, North Carolina, dumped banana-scented deodorant into Three Mile Branch stream.

✳

The Mary E. Cunningham Award for Promoting the Image of Women in Business to:

Jodi Stutz, a twenty-one-year-old secretary at Deere & Company in Moline, Illinois, who was fired in 1980 for making a Xerox copy of her bottom.

How Could They Tell?

In his first twenty months in office, President Reagan took nearly sixteen weeks' vacation.

15

JUST A LITTLE NAUSEATED

1966 Mrs. Myra Franklin of Cardiff, Wales, saw the movie *The Sound of Music* five hundred times. "I'm never bored," she said.

YOU DON'T WANT TO KNOW WHAT THE ONES SENT TO SAN FRANCISCO ARE USED FOR

1980 Baxters, a soup manufacturer in northern Scotland, reported an inexplicable upsurge in demand for pizzles—the private parts of male deer—fifteen thousand of which were shipped abroad last year. Those sent to the Orient are believed to be used in medicines.

✳

HAND JOB OF THE YEAR

1981 Nancy Reagan summoned her Los Angeles manicurist to the capital to do her nails for the President's seventieth-birthday celebration.

✳

ESQUIRE'S ANNUAL MELON NEWS ROUNDUP: 1979

KGB agents in Tsodniskari, USSR, were called in to investigate the theft of twenty thousand pounds of melons from a collective farm.

Ivan Bright of Hope, Arkansas, almost won the $10,000 prize offered to anyone who could grow a two-hundred-pound watermelon. The contest, sponsored by a local booster organization, had a deadline of midnight on Friday, but Bright's melon didn't hit two hundred pounds until Sunday.

Tomoyuki Ono, a Tokyo graphics designer, cultivated a cubic watermelon (seven inches by seven inches by seven inches), and two of Tokyo's leading department stores sold the melons at $19.95 apiece. Ono said, "My main object is to market them as art."

✳

Here's to Those Who Chill 'Em, Swill 'Em, and Stick 'Em Together

1982 With the thousands of beer cans he had collected as a hobby for fifteen years, John Milkovisch, sixty-nine, of Houston, built a beer-can shroud around his home.

A MAN IS MUGGED IN PASSAIC, NEW JERSEY, EVERY TWENTY MINUTES. THIS IS HIS STORY

Between 1972 and 1977 Mike Maryn of Passaic, New Jersey, fifty-six, was mugged eighty-three times. He was hospitalized at least twenty times. He was stabbed, shot at twice, and hit over the head with a pipe. His ear was partly cut off, his nose broken, his ribs kicked in, his teeth knocked out, and his skull fractured. He lost more than $2,000 in cash and several bags of groceries. Four of his cars were stolen. Police offered him a walkie-talkie so he could signal for help, but he declined. "It would only be taken from me," he said.

*

WHAT A DISH

1981 Nancy Reagan ordered 220 place settings of White House china at a cost of $209,508 (given by a private donor). Said Mrs. Reagan: "The White House really badly, badly needs china."

*

GODZILLA, WE'VE GOT TO STOP MEETING LIKE THIS

1975 The City Council of Stanfield, Oregon, passed a law prohibiting animals from having sex in public.

*

Pull Up 932 Chairs, Fellas, and Sit Down

1970 Benny and Billy McCrary of Hendersonville, North Carolina, weighed 660 and 640 pounds respectively, wore size 14 and 15EEE shoes, and were the largest twins in the world.

WE DON'T HEAR YOU APPLAUDING FOR...

1975 Mark Pauga broke the world rocking-chair record in Lombard, Illinois. He rocked for 336 hours.

1975 David Chabira and John Benaka broke the world Ferris-wheel-riding record at Joyland Park Amusement Park, Topeka, Kansas. They rode for 22 days, 4 hours, 2 minutes.

WHICH WORKS OUT TO A 10,080-PACK-A-DAY HABIT

1983 Jim Purol of Livonia, Michigan, smoked seven packs of cigarettes in sixty seconds on a local television show.

It's a Dirty, Rotten, Lousy Job — but Somebody's Gotta Do It

1980 Ann Getty, wife of one of J. Paul Getty's sons, spent $77,000 at Saks Fifth Avenue during the year, making her the store's best private customer.

IN AMERICA, WE'RE NOT SO CHOOSY. JUST GIVE US A LITTLE ONION DIP AND THE SEAT

1978 Frenchman Michel Lotito, known as Monsieur Mangetout, broke his own record by eating fifteen pounds of bicycle. He said the chain was the best part because it had "taste."

✳

UNFORTUNATELY IT'S IN GREEK

1981 The Aeolus Company announced the marketing of an aerosol spray that gives men "instant sex appeal." Containing a secret ingredient derived from testosterone, the spray, according to Aeolus president Bill Williams, aids a man by sending off "a powerful subconscious message to a woman."

✳

IT'S 10 P.M. DO YOU KNOW WHERE YOUR PARRAKEET IS?

1975 New York police, investigating a disturbance inside a parked car, arrested a thirty-four-year-old man from Wichita, Kansas, on charges of sodomy with a duck.

✳

Mommy, Mommy, Can We Ride the Dalai Lama Again?

1979 The International Society for Krishna Consciousness opened an ornate Indian palace in the foothills of rural West Virginia, which they planned to make the centerpiece of a "religious Disneyland" called Krishnaland.

THEREBY BREAKING THE HEARTS OF THE CITY'S PIGEONS

1981 The Philadelphia Art Commission declined to accept Sylvester Stallone's donation of an eight-and-a-half-foot statue of himself, offered on the condition that it stand at the top of the steps outside the Philadelphia Museum of Art.

So What's a Few Hours of Happiness After Centuries of Persecution?

1978 Stanford Cohen of Miami rented the Orange Bowl to hold a bar mitzvah party for his son Harvey. The celebration included three hundred friends, a hundred-member high school marching band, majorettes, waiters dressed as referees, and waitresses dressed as cheerleaders. The scoreboard flashed HAPPY BIRTHDAY, HARVEY.

BUT NO TICKEE, NO MONEE

1980 Jeeves, a dry-cleaning shop on New York's Madison Avenue, offered to press customers' wrinkled cash at no extra charge.

*

AFTER THAT, IT WAS INTO THE WOODSHED FOR CIGARS AND COGNAC

1978 After asking what he was eating for dinner at the house of his father-in-law, Argentinian Amaro Maturano was told the dish was roast dog. Maturano then went outside and strangled forty chickens, killed nine mules and three cows, then set fire to a truck and a farmhouse.

*

THEN HOW COME WE GOT THESE NUTS IN OUR HERSHEY BAR?

1972 The Food and Drug Administration's limits on foreign matter that can legally be contained in processed food included: an average of fifty insect fragments or two rodent hairs per hundred grams of peanut butter; for tomato juice, ten fruit-fly eggs or two larvae in the same amount.

*

THIS LAWN ISN'T BIG ENOUGH FOR THE TWO OF US

1981 Frank Karnes, thirty-nine, of Sacramento, California, pulled a gun and shot his power mower because it wouldn't start.

*

Awww!

1983 As Houston socialite Carolyn Farb showed a *People* magazine reporter her six-room closet, which holds her wardrobe of some one thousand pieces worth more than $750,000, she commented: "I hope this isn't poking fun at all of this. I mean, look at what they did to poor Nancy Reagan."

Join the Navy.
No Cover.
No Minimum.

1975 Commander Connelly Stevenson was relieved of his command after he allowed go-go dancer Cat Futch to perform topless aboard his nuclear submarine.

Heart Doc to Give Head to Housewife?

1979 The *National Enquirer* offered Dr. Christiaan Barnard $250,000 to perform a human head transplant.

AND LIVED!

25

**LGE. STUDIO, FURN.,
PARKING ON PREMISES,
NO PETS**

1980 John Barbeck lost control of his station wagon, which ran through a yard in south Chicago and rammed into Frank Wisniewski's basement.

✳

**A GOOD SAND,
BUT NOT A GREAT SAND**

1968 Mrs. Martha Jacobs of Pretoria, South Africa, couldn't stop eating sand. When she moved away from her home town, she said, "I just couldn't get any decent eating sand in Natal. I had to write to my brother in Pretoria to send me some. It wasn't long before three pounds of genuine Transvaal sand arrived in the post. I started eating the moment I got the packet." Afterward she got her husband to bring home sand for her. Her doctor said it wouldn't hurt her.

✳

**WE JUST TIE OURS
TO A DOORKNOB
AND SLAM THE DOOR**

1975 Los Angeles women began using Preparation H on their faces to shrink bags under their eyes.

✳

TOP *THAT*, JERRY LEWIS!

1978 Brian Reif, seventeen, ate eighty-two worms in Bradford, Ontario, in a fund-raising stunt for muscular dystrophy.

✳

Overreachers

1976 To counteract adverse publicity, Pennsylvania governor Milton J. Shapp lunched at Philadelphia's Bellevue Stratford, site of the ill-fated American Legion convention.

1981 New York governor Hugh Carey responded to critics of a contaminated state office building in Binghamton by offering to drink a glassful of PCBs.

The Runner Bumbles

1978 Dennis Rainear was shot in the head at the ten-mile mark of a Michigan marathon. He finished the race, saying afterward, "I was sure I could knock thirty-one seconds off my time, and then this silly thing had to happen."

ONE MAN, ONE VOLT

1972 Senator Thomas Eagleton (D-Mo.) accepted the Vice-Presidential nomination without telling Presidential nominee George McGovern that he had undergone electric shock therapy.

AND LIVED!

BOSS, I KNOW YOU'RE NOT GOING TO BELIEVE THIS, BUT THE REASON I WAS LATE TO WORK THIS MORNING WAS...

1968 A man driving along New York's Grand Central Parkway one morning was struck by a three-foot kangaroo in midhop. The car and driver survived the encounter, but the kangaroo didn't. None of the Port Authority police could guess where it came from, nor could they prove the incident occurred, since no pictures were taken and the kangaroo was disposed of in Flushing Bay.

✳

ESOPHAGUS NOW

1979 After Dick Winslow appeared at Good Samaritan Hospital in Los Angeles complaining of pain in his throat, doctors found a Mickey Mouse watch lodged in his esophagus. Winslow said the watch must have been in a glass of vitamin pills he had swallowed several days earlier.

✳

CONDIMENTS IN THE NEWS

1980 A UPS truck in Lansing, Michigan, was stolen by three young women who had taken off all their clothes and covered their bodies with mustard.

Rip Howell, a student at the University of Southwestern Louisiana, sat in a keg of ketchup for seventeen and one-half hours.

✳

BUT HAVE YOU TRIED MRS. ROTH'S POTATO KUGEL?

1970 Surinder Maini, an Indian nature-care doctor, announced that he eats a brick a day.

✳

Bang, Bang, You're Deaf

1982 Officer Ralph McNail of the St. Louis Police Department stuck bullets in his ears to deaden the noise of an Elton John concert.

Hey, Bister, Wadda See By Dids?

1975 San Francisco show girl Brandy Corbin underwent fifteen acupuncture treatments that increased her bust measurement from thirty-five to forty inches and also cured a slight cold.

BELIEVE IT OR NOT, WILLIAM HALL DRILLED SEVEN HOLES IN HIS HEAD WITH A POWER DRILL... AND LIVED!

1982 William G. Hall of Shrewsbury, England, killed himself by drilling eight holes in his head with a power drill.

∗

A DINER'S GUIDE TO TRENTON, NEW JERSEY

1981 William Cook, forty-six, of Trenton, was indicted for assaulting George Sabatino, nineteen, his daughter's boyfriend. Cook bit off the front of Sabatino's nose.

Herbert Lemon, also of Trenton, was charged with biting off the eyebrow of his girlfriend, Hazel Warner, after she tried to stop him from shooting Elaine Flowers.

∗

GIVE YOURSELF A SECOND OR TWO

1983 A number of New York City youngsters were found to be stealing subway tokens by sucking them from the turnstile slots. Said Hugh A. Dunne of the Transit Authority, "The kids quickly come with their mouths and suck it right up. I frankly couldn't think of anything more downright unhealthy."

∗

BUT FOR HEMORRHOIDS, THE OLD DOORKNOB-AND-STRING TRICK STILL WORKS BEST

1977 Uruguayan farmer Ernesto Erosa wanted to end the tormenting pain of a toothache and so shot away the tooth with a .22-caliber pistol. He destroyed the tooth, his gums, his lower lip and jaw.

∗

AND LIVED!

An Honest Mistake

1972 While attending the opening ceremonies for a new office building, Cleveland mayor Ralph J. Perk set fire to his hair with a welding torch.

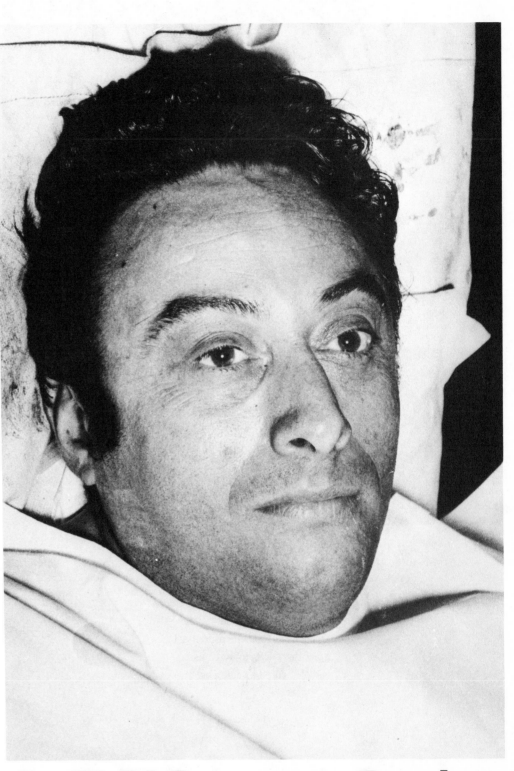

An El Al Courtesy Card to:

Lenny Bruce, who in 1965 fell out a San Francisco hotel window while doing an imitation of what he called Superjew. He suffered back injuries and broke an arm.

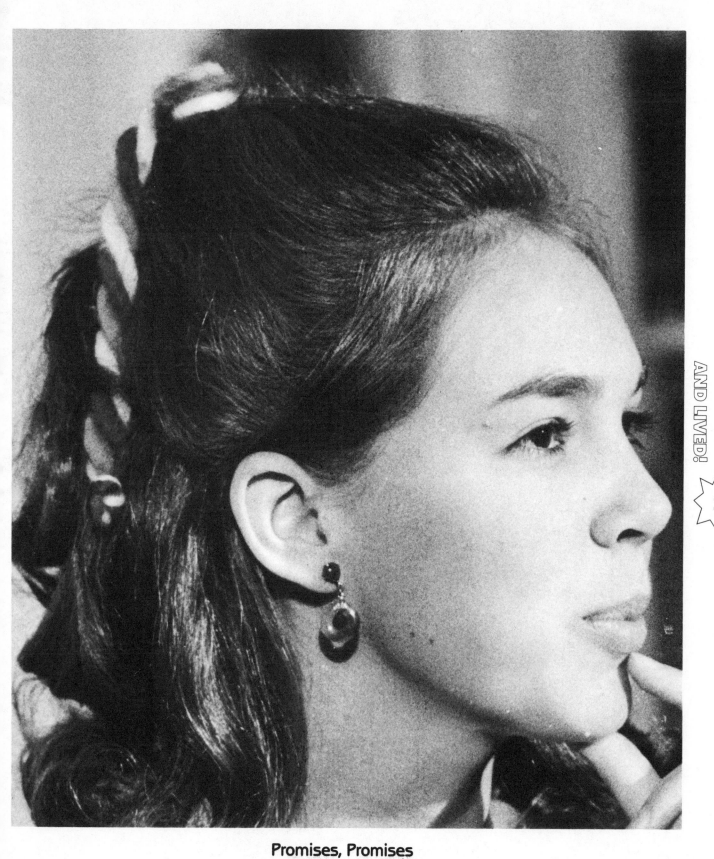

Promises, Promises

1972 While campaigning for her father in Columbus, Ohio, Julie Nixon Eisenhower said that she would die for the Thieu regime.

CHEAP SHOTS

Best New Face
of 1982: Pia Zadora

WORST PUBLICITY BREAK FOR
ELIZABETH TAYLOR AND GINA LOLLABRIGIDA
1961 They met in Moscow,
wearing the same dress.

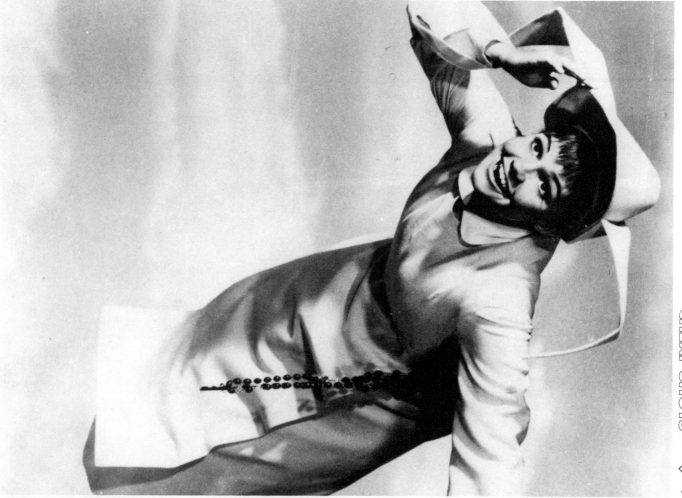

Copilot of 1968

Sally Field, star of *The Flying Nun,* announced her belief that her television role had led her back to God.

LITTLE BIG MENSCH

1980 Henny Youngman, seventy-three, was bar mitzvahed, sixty years after his ceremony was postponed due to a death in the family.

**1973 Lester Maddox (Top)
Rides Mule (Bottom)
While Spectators (Left
and Right) Look On**

LESTER G. MADDOX
GOVERNOR

OVA-REACHUH

1968 Lester Maddox offered himself as a candidate for the Presidency of the United States.

Y'All Come Back, Hair?
Lester Maddox, before and after February 1972

TRUE GRITS

1970 Lester Maddox...fingered his son for suspicion of burglary, remarking on the event: "It was a painful thing.... I could see his little old head sitting up in the back of the car as they drove off."

...offered to ride on top of that train carrying lethal nerve gas through Georgia to show it was perfectly safe. The Army declined his offer and used rabbits instead.

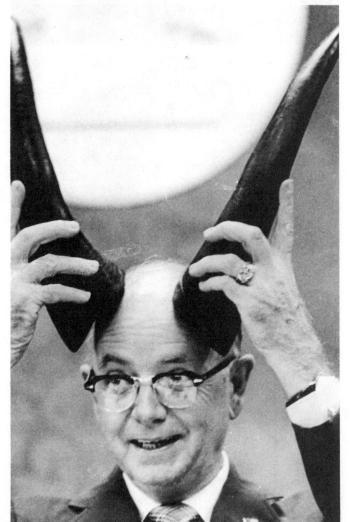

Dumbest Controversy of 1964

Topless bathing suits

Dumbest Solution to Dumbest Controversy of 1964

John Frederics's hat with flaps that lower to cover the girl in a topless bathing suit

Primate of the Century: Billy Carter

NOW, THAT'SA FUNNY!

1979 During a memorial service for Aldo Moro, retired Christian Democrat Angelo Gallo grabbed and twisted the ears of party member Amintore Fanfani because he "wasn't tough enough on communism."

Watch It, Fella— uh, Bella

1981 "We need laws that protect everyone," boomed Bella Abzug at an ERA rally in San Francisco, "men and women, straights and gays, regardless of sexual perversion—uh, persuasion."

Statesman of 1968

Prime Minister Pierre Trudeau of Canada accepts the necktie given him as honorary member of the National Press Club in Ottawa.

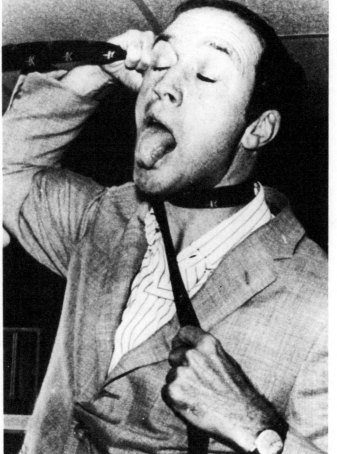

DEAR MR. PYNCHON: AS YOU KNOW, I'VE BEEN ASKED TO TIE UP A FEW
LOOSE ENDS IN YOUR ADORABLE NEW BOOK. (MY, IT'S A FAT MASTERPIECE!)
AS YOU CAN SEE, I'VE MADE A FEW TEENSY PENCIL MARKS, ONE ON
PAGE SIX, THE OTHER ON PAGE SEVEN. THE REST LOOKS SUBLIME...

1975 Jacqueline Onassis was
hired as an editor by Viking
Press.

Just So He Shouldn't Starve

1965 On the occasion of Pope Paul's visit to the U.S. in October, the Sixth Avenue Delicatessen in New York packed a snack of bagels, cream cheese, and lox for the pope's homeward flight. The brown-paper package was marked FOR HIS HOLY HIGHNESS.

Neither Was the Triboro Bridge

1972 Upon unveiling his portrait of the President, Norman Rockwell said Nixon "was no fun to paint."

"LET ME SAY THIS ABOUT THAT. WE'VE GOT TO GET THIS COUNTRY HOPPING AGAIN."

FINALLY! A SELECTION OF YARMULKES FOR THE REALLY ACTIVE MAN

Why Is This Man Limping?

The Latest in Speed-trap Hiding Places

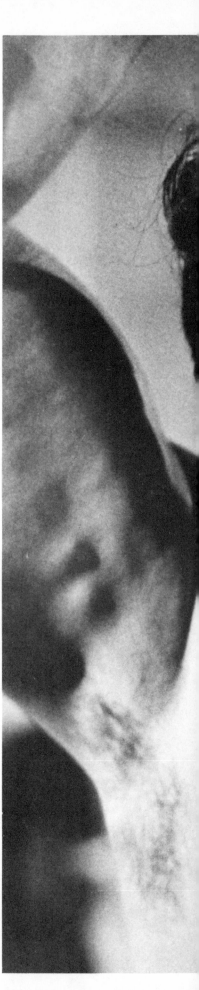

Out of the Jeans of Babes

1981 In the July *Ladies' Home Journal,* Brooke Shields admitted that she had kissed boys but denied that she had ever been sexually aroused—"at least I don't think so," she said. "I believe I'll know it when I feel it."

Offering herself as a spokesperson for a government antismoking campaign, Brooke Shields explained, "Smoking kills. If you're killed, you've lost a very important part of your life."

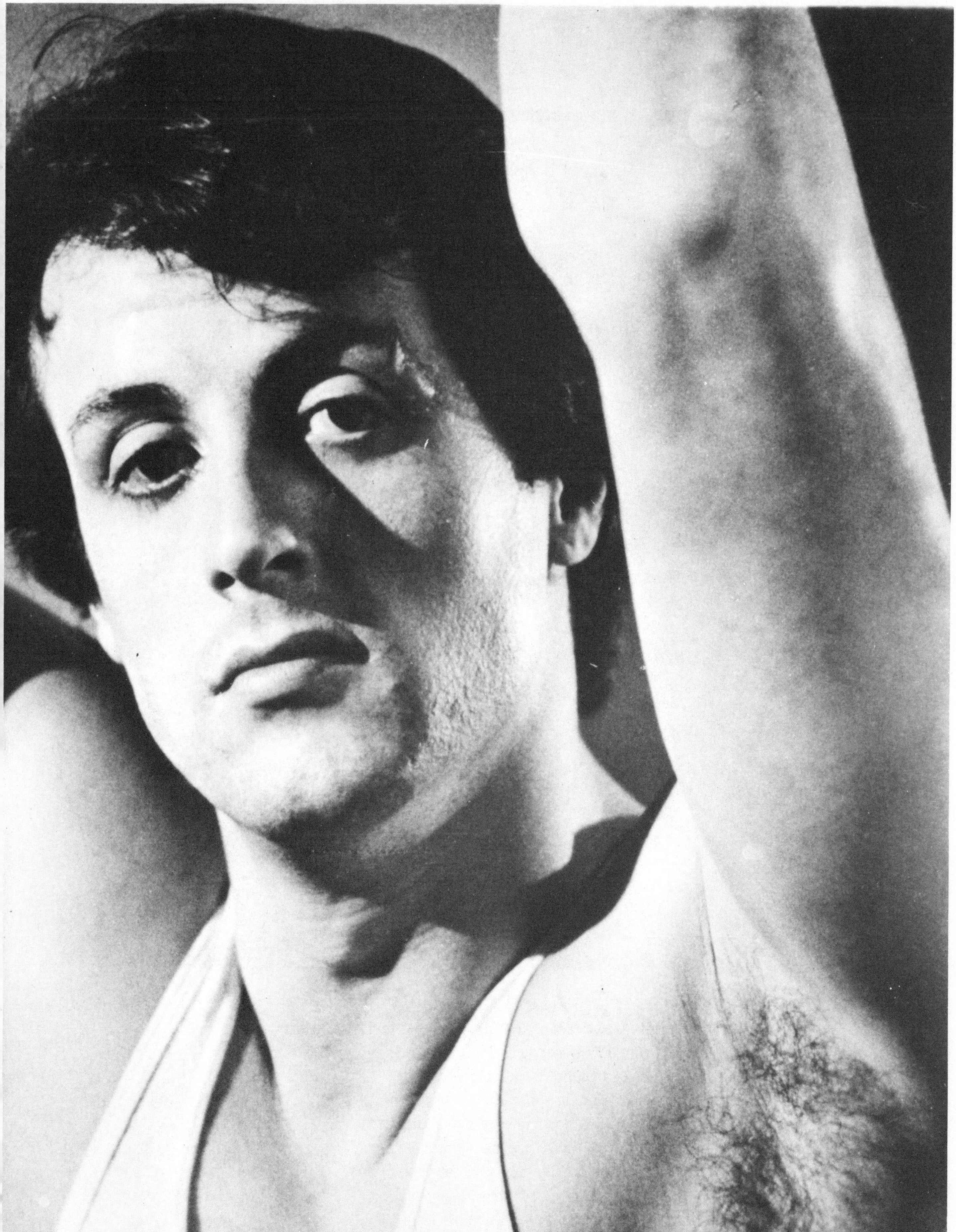

You Call That Proof?

1978 Margaux Hemingway spent two weeks in the Amazon jungle in Venezuela shooting an ABC documentary about the Makiritare Indians. Margaux said of the local tribesmen: "I was the first white woman in the camp. They wanted to touch my breasts to prove I wasn't a man."

Ash Hole of 1980

Mount St. Helens

YEAH, AND THE VENUS DE MILO HAD LEPROSY

1975 Dr. Finn Becker-Christiansen of Copenhagen diagnosed the secret of the *Mona Lisa* smile: congenital facial palsy.

The Wham, Bam, Thank You Ma'am Prize

1963 Time allotted to Metropolitan Museum of Art visitors to look at the *Mona Lisa:* ten seconds

Opera Buff
of 1973

Soprano Carol Neblett totally disrobed during the first act of a performance of Massenet's *Thaïs*.

LIABILITY
OR
COLLISION?

1974 Edy Williams insured her
breasts for $1 million.

A Man for All Seasonings

1983 Eight months after launching Newman's Own Oil and Vinegar Salad Dressing, Paul Newman introduced his Industrial Strength Venetian Spaghetti Sauce.

Sorest Loser of 1962

David Merrick responded to the New York critics' panning of his show *Subways Are for Sleeping* by finding seven men with the same names as the critics and publishing an ad featuring rave quotes from the seven.

The Politics of Joy

1968 Mrs. Hubert Humphrey reacted too slowly in turning down a piece of cake offered her by Mrs. Joseph Barr, wife of the Pittsburgh mayor.

Hire the Handicapped and They'll Work It Out

1970 Minnesota Twin Frank Quilici raised his batting average to .370 by changing his stance so he could see around his nose.

CHEAP SHOTS

54

It Is Not Development, It Is Megalopolis

1974 Explaining that there was no need for her to diet, Anita Ekberg said, "It is not fatness. It is development."

LET ME ENTERTAIN YOU...

LET ME MAKE YOU SMILE...

LET ME DO A FEW TRICKS...

SOME OLD AND THEN SOME
NEW TRICKS...

I'M VERY VERSATILE!

TO SAY NOTHING OF YOUR HAIRCUT, YOUR SUITS, YOUR VOICE, YOUR NAME, YOUR EARS, YOUR SON, YOUR SON'S BAND, YOUR REPUTATION IN FRANCE...

1980 Jerry Lewis told *Los Angeles* magazine that the reason many people hated him was that he was a "multifaceted, talented, wealthy, internationally famous genius."

One Lifetime MacArthur Foundation Grant to:

Twiggy for the following exchange in 1967:

Twiggy: Churchill? I remember him. I don't really know what it was he did, but he was an adorable old man, a really decent old man—a pity he died....

Reporter: Twiggy, do you know what happened at Hiroshima?

Twiggy: Where's that?

Reporter: In Japan.

Twiggy: No. I've never heard of it. What happened there?

Reporter: A hundred thousand people died on the spot.

Twiggy: Oh, God! When did you say it happened? Where? Hiroshima? But that's ghastly. A hundred thousand dead? It's frightful. Men are mad.

Bert Parks Wept

Debra Sue Maffett, Miss America of 1982, was discovered to have had a nose job in 1980.

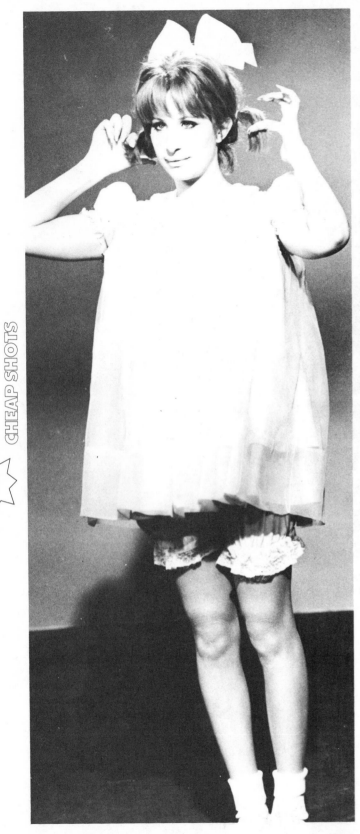

Well?

1978 A State Department spokesman, explaining why an oil portrait of Henry Kissinger was rejected, said the picture portrayed Kissinger as "a dwarf, a rogues' gallery thing."

May the Dalai Lama Leave a Gift in Your Hookah

1971 Barbra Streisand revealed she smoked marijuana while performing in a Las Vegas nightclub act because "it relieved all my tensions."

Yenta, Heal Thyself

1975 Ann Landers announced that she was getting a divorce.

HERE'S YOUR HAT, WHAT'S YOUR HURRY?

1980 In an interview with *The New York Times*, Ronald Reagan promised to resign from the Presidency if he ever went senile.

60

Sportsmen of 1963

Dean Rusk and Nikita Khrushchev paused in their top-level conference on the fate of the world to play a grueling set of badminton. Rusk lost.

OLD GOLFERS NEVER DIE...

1964 The following statements were made by Dwight D. Eisenhower this election year:

1. Before the Republican Convention: "I am showing no partiality to anyone.... I've been completely consistent in this and I have double-crossed no one."

2. At the Republican Convention: "It would be very hard to say what my role is or even what I think my role is."

3. After the Republican Convention: "The campaign is getting to be a confused state of affairs. I can't define the issues."

Once in a Very Great While, a Woman Comes Along Who Shakes the Conscience of a Nation: Harriet Tubman, Susan B. Anthony, Eleanor Roosevelt, and Now...

1979 Debbie Shook tried to destroy the crown she wore as Miss North Carolina 1978. Shook was stripped of her title after she complained that she hadn't received all the prizes due her.

In This Corner, at 255 Pounds, in Extra-Large Trunks…

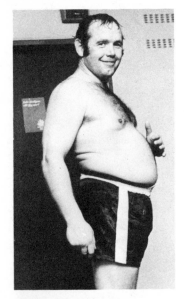

1969 Ingemar Johansson announced he was planning a comeback.

ENDLESS NOSH

1982 Sculptor Dwight Kalb crafted a chopped-liver statue of Brooke Shields for Mel Markon's, a Chicago restaurant.

A TUBE OF CLEARASIL—
A BIG TUBE—TO:

Jerry Rubin of the Yippies, who
said in 1968, "My goal is at the
age of thirty-five to act like I'm
fifteen."

And in This Corner, Wearing a White Satin Tarpaulin...

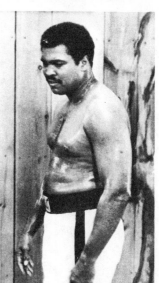

1979 Following a ten-round
exhibition fight in Ghent, Bel-
gium, Muhammad Ali apol-
ogized to fans for the shape he
was in.

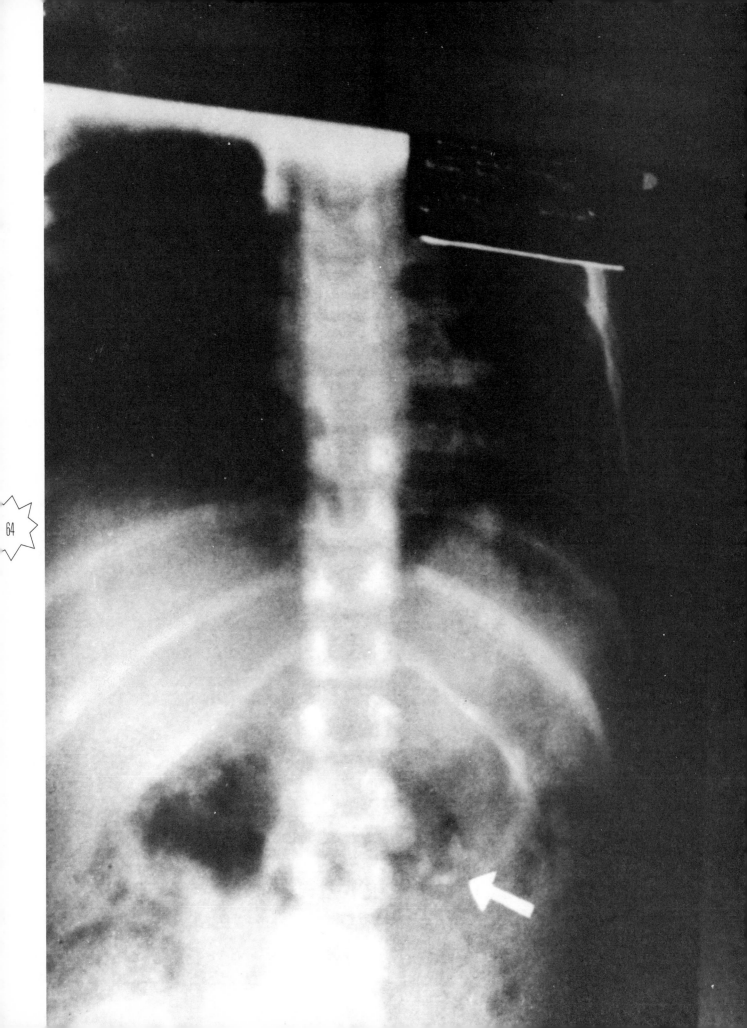

FRONTIERS OF KNOWLEDGE

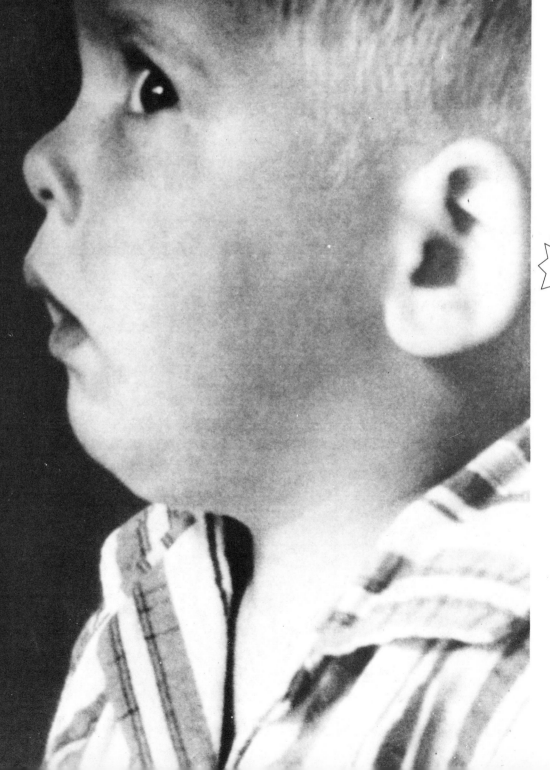

THOUGH NOT EXACTLY JUMPING FOR JOY

1968 Two-year-old Brad Haines swallowed whole his pet turtle, Myrtle. Although he complained of no pain, the doctors X-rayed him, revealing Myrtle in his stomach, very much alive.

✳

FOUR MEDITERRANEAN FRUIT FLIES MAGNIFIED TWO HUNDRED TIMES

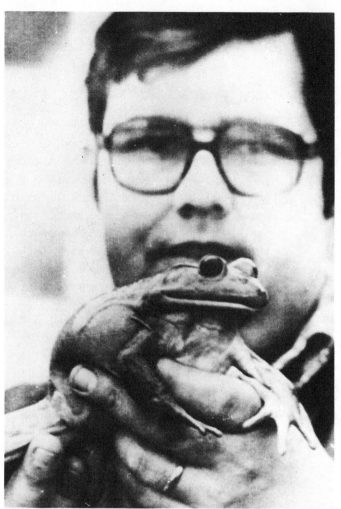

Kind of Like Georgie Jessel

1980 Biologists at the University of Prince Edward Island discovered a frog that makes a *meow* sound instead of croaking.

HOLD IT A MINUTE, BUCKY. WE GOT THE NOBEL COMMITTEE ON THE LINE RIGHT NOW

1973 Buckminster Fuller revealed his secret for avoiding getting cold on an airplane: he said he stuffed a newspaper inside his suit.

✳

WHATEVER MAKES THEM HAPPY

1981 A study at the Aegean University in Ankara, Turkey, revealed that disco music causes homosexuality in mice.

✳

THE ONE WITHOUT A HOLE DIDN'T WORK

1975 The British government, questioning the adequacy of conventional toilet seats, conducted secret studies in which men and women were photographed on a variety of experimental models.

✳

For Sale: '79 Kid, Good Cond., Leaks

1980 James and Pamela Green of Frenchtown, New Jersey, were arrested for trying to trade their fourteen-month-old son, James Junior, for a 1977 black and silver Corvette.

**ALL OUR BEAGLES
WEAR METHYL
P-HYDROXYBENZOATE
OR THEY WEAR
NOTHING AT ALL**

1979 Three Purdue University scientists announced their discovery that methyl p-hydroxybenzoate, a chemical commonly used in food preservatives, cosmetics, and perfume, sexually excites beagles.

*

**FOR THIS I SENT YOU
FOUR YEARS
TO MEDICAL SCHOOL?**

1978 Researchers at the Mount Sinai Medical Center in Miami Beach found that chicken soup is an "efficacious upper respiratory tract infection therapy."

*

You Salvage the Twentieth Century; We've Had It

1968 A Los Angeles engineer revealed this vision of the American woman in the year 2000: Body paint and makeup would provide mineral insulation against the weather, air pollutants, and radioactivity; a computer necklace would program her household; her hat would act as receiver and transmitter for a two-way radio worn around her arms; her jewelry would double as warning devices; and her earrings would provide power for all components.

YOU RANG?

1980 Koko, the "talking" gorilla, who communicates with humans by using sign language, called her trainer "panty toilet dirty devil."

BOYSENBERRY TO PRUNE, BOYSENBERRY TO PRUNE: DO YOU READ ME?

1975 Lie-detector expert Cleve Backster reported to the annual meeting of the American Association for the Advancement of Science that he had detected electrical impulses between two containers of yogurt at opposite ends of his laboratory. Backster claimed the bacteria in the containers were communicating.

✶

AND THEY STILL HAVEN'T FOUND A CURE FOR MAMBO HEMORRHOIDS

1979 Dr. Frederick Walker of the Johns Hopkins Hospital reported the first known case of "disco felon" in *The New England Journal of Medicine*. "Felon" is a disease characterized by a painful inflammation of the fingertips, caused in this case by snapping the fingers to music.

✶

BUT THEY'RE INSUFFERABLE BOARS AT PARTIES

1980 Jogging pigs, used by researchers at Arizona State University to study heart problems, were found to be more energetic as well as more cheerful than nonjogging pigs.

✶

WOODY THAT IT WERE TRUE

1979 The editors of *Chemical and Engineering News* reported in error that a woodpecker's beak strikes a tree at an impact velocity of 1,300 miles per hour. At that velocity, the woodpecker's head would break the sound barrier twice as it bounced against the tree.

✶

So That's Why They're Never Around When We Need Them

1963 Dr. Charles R. Warren of the United States Geological Survey revealed that the moon probably is covered with fuzz.

WE SEE YOUR NINE HEARTS AND THREE LIVERS AND RAISE YOU THREE GIZZARDS

1976 A chicken cooked in Dnepropetrovsk, near Kiev, was found to have nine hearts and three livers.

∗

AT LAST, SOMETHING THAT DOESN'T CAUSE CANCER

1980 Dr. Rai Antic of the Royal Adelaide Hospital in Australia claimed that snoring can cause heart attacks, mental illness, and death.

∗

SOVIETS DISCOVER LAWYERS IN SPACE

1981 Russian scientists concluded that if intelligent life exists on other planets, it is most likely in the form of highly active tailless lizards.

∗

ALAS, POOR ELVIS, HE DIED TOO SOON

1982 A study by Dr. David Margules of Temple University found that given a drug called naloxone, obese, impotent mice fed a steady diet of sweets will turn into "svelt studs."

∗

GOOD!

1979 Four Swedish scientists at the University of Lund discovered that earthworms feel pain.

∗

BETTER!

1980 A three-year study in Britain concluded that fish, when hooked, actually do feel pain.

∗

BETTER YET!

1971 According to a study conducted by Dr. Frederick Urbach of Temple University, fish get sunburned.

∗

HERPES VIRUS MAGNIFIED THREE MILLION TIMES

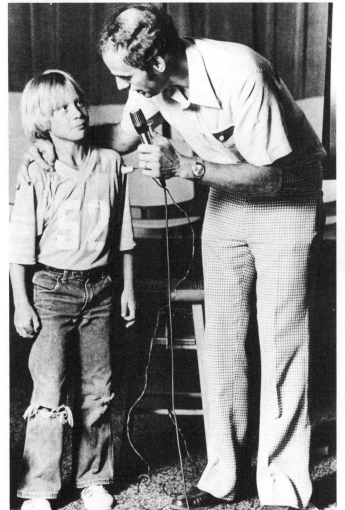

Juice for Jesus

1981 The Reverend Dwight Wymer, a Baptist minister, used a twelve-volt battery to shock his students as he delivered his message at a Bible school in Grand Rapids. Wymer said: "God tells us to do something or suffer the consequences. When we don't do it, zap!"

Follow Harold Bate's Car, but Not Too Closely

1973 Harold Bate of Totnes, England, invented a device to distill the manure of pigs, cattle, chickens, dogs, or humans into fuel for automobiles. One hundred pounds of pig manure, he said, would produce about eight gallons of "very high performance stuff."

FRONTIERS OF KNOWLEDGE

**SOUNDS LIKE THE GIRL
WE TOOK TO OUR PROM**

1981 Syracuse, New York, orthodontist David Marshall contended that as a result of today's diet of soft, processed foods and the fact that we no longer use our teeth as weapons, our descendants will have fewer teeth, much smaller jaws, and a much more prominent nose and chin, and will be practically hairless.

✳

**SOMETIMES YOU FEEL
LIKE A NUT...**

1980 John McLoughlin, a Long Island high school teacher, was suspended for leaving a five-inch tarantula in a candy dish on his department chairman's desk.

✳

**MOTHER OF MERCY,
IS THIS THE END
OF MEL BROOKS?**

1979 Dr. Brent Skura of the University of British Columbia attempted to develop the gasless bean. Skura said he would consider it a significant dietary breakthrough if he could provide the world with a nutritious bean that would not cause its eaters subsequent embarrassment.

✳

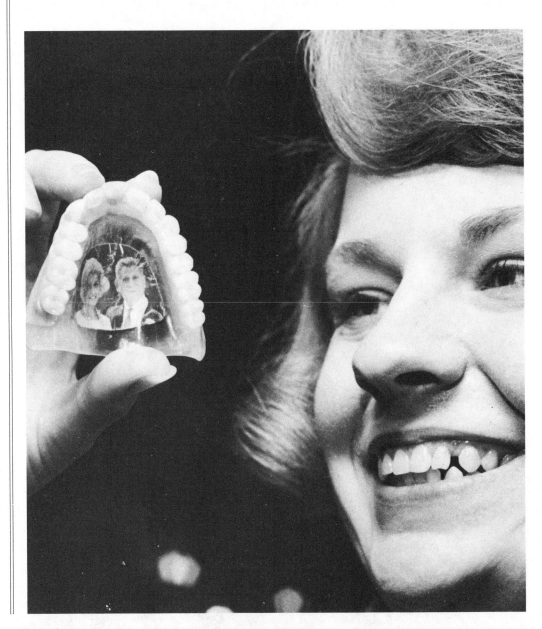

ADVERTISEMENTS FOR MYSELF

1967 Demonstrated at the Chicago Dental Society meeting were dentures in which a photo of the wearer was embedded for identification in emergencies.

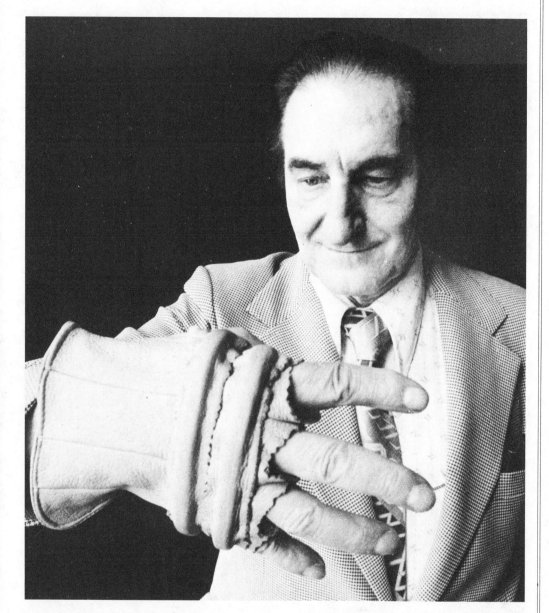

What's He Got for Kissing Babies?

1975 Anthony Monde of Reading, Pennsylvania, invented a glove for politicians who do a lot of hand shaking. The glove has a metal rib construction that protects the hand from strong grips and wrist twisting.

JUST SO THEY DON'T GRAFT SHECKY GREEN ONTO OUR CHICKEN
1976 Dr. Eleanor Storrs received the Charles A. Griffin award from the American Association for Laboratory Animal Science for successfully transmitting human leprosy to an armadillo.

✳

ISS GOOD BUT STINK
1982 Archaeologists in York, England, found a piece of dirty laundry that they believe to have been the wool sock of a Viking warrior one thousand years ago.

✳

GENDER GAP UPDATE
1981 According to a study by Steven Fischer and Ralph Turner of the University of Pennsylvania, the top ten female fears are fire, dead people, feeling rejected, mice or rats, failure, hurting the feelings of others, weapons, surgery, speaking in public, and looking down from tall buildings. For men: Speaking in public, failure, hurting people's feelings, looking foolish, falling, being rejected, surgery, being disapproved of, being criticized, and bats.

✳

IT'S CALLED THE DR. JOYCE BROTHERS
1977 An agricultural research group developed a square tomato.

✳

BUT IT STILL REMEMBERS CHAPPAQUIDDICK
1979 Princeton University memory researchers reported the successful breeding of an amnesic fruit fly, which forgets odors four times as quickly as a normal fruit fly.

✳

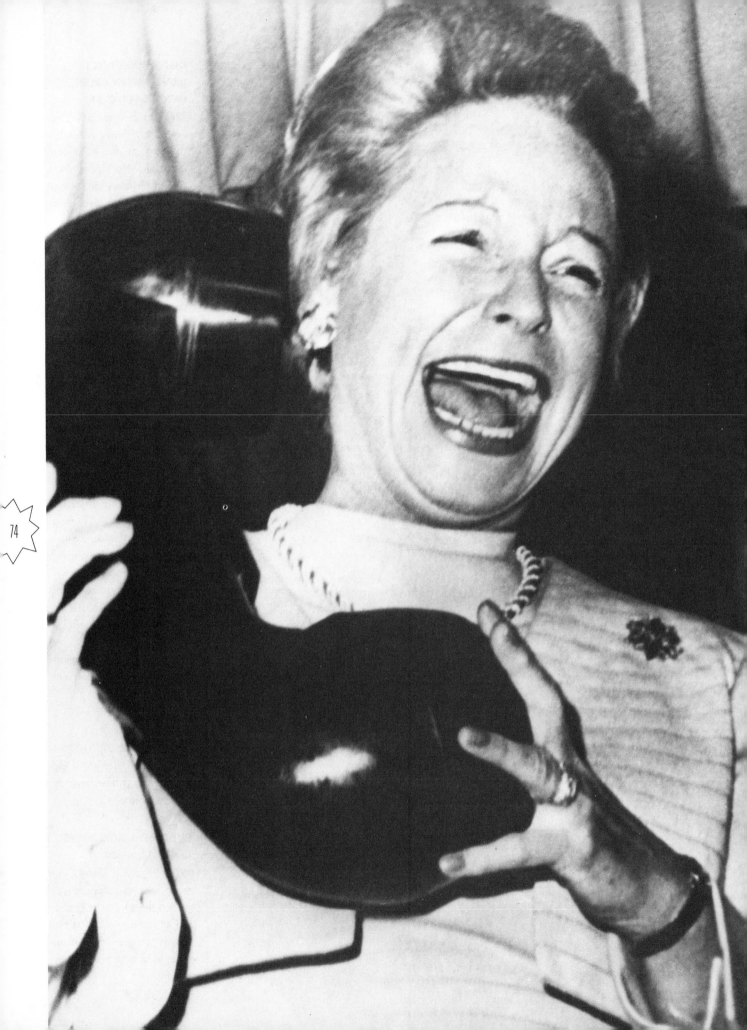

WORDS WITHOUT BRAINS

BUT DON'T EVERYBODY JUMP UP AT ONCE

1972 Speaking at the Midwest Republican Women's Conference, Martha Mitchell said, "Everybody should rise up and say, 'Thank you, Mr. President, for bombing Haiphong.'"

∗

QUICK, CLOSE THE WINDOW! I JUST MOPPED THE FLOOR, AND UNCLE HESHIE IS COMING OVER IN FIVE MINUTES

1980 Sid Goldstein, a New York entrepreneur, proposed flying human ashes to the troposphere, then releasing them into the jet stream. Goldstein, whose earlier proposal to inter human ashes on the moon had been rejected by NASA, said: "The jet stream idea is better. This way, you've got the altitude, plus you can pass over your home and loved ones every twenty hours."

∗

HO, HO, HO. UNCLE HESHIE IN BUTTER SAUCE

1980 The Southwestern Bell Company's Yellow Pages listed the Elliot-Hamil Funeral Home under "wholesale frozen foods."

∗

JUST HOLD STILL

1982 Roy Rogers was recruited by the National Rifle Association to fight a California referendum to restrict handguns. Said Rogers, "They'll have to shoot me first to take my gun."

∗

Is That a Nightstick in Your Pocket, or Are You Just Glad to See Me?

1971 Philadelphia police commissioner Frank Rizzo was elected mayor on a strong anticrime platform. "I'm gonna be so tough as a mayor," Rizzo promised, "I'm gonna make Attila the Hun look like a faggot."

**PEE-IN-TOILET
SWIM-IN-POOL**

1973 Asked who wrote his speeches, Olympic medalist Mark Spitz replied, "Having a speech writer would be definitely too plastic. I just try to remember six key words before every talk."

✻

OH, SHUT UP

1968 Jill Johnston in *The Village Voice:* "Telling it like it is means telling it like it was and how it is now that it isn't what it was to the is now people."

✻

**IF YOU'RE HAPPY,
WE'RE HAPPY**

1977 On entering prison at Maxwell Air Force Base, John Mitchell said, "It's nice to be back in Alabama." On returning to Calhoun, Georgia, after his resignation, Bert Lance said, "It's nice to be back in Georgia."

✻

JESUS WEPT

1971 Grace Slick of the Jefferson Airplane officially named her daughter "god." Why the small *g*? "Because we've got to be humble about this," said the singer.

At Last, an Original Idea

1974 Commenting on the SLA's demand of free food for the poor in exchange for the release of Patty Hearst, California governor Ronald Reagan said, "It's just too bad we can't have an epidemic of botulism."

1982: CELEBRATING THE SEVENTEENTH ANNIVERSARY OF THE MARCH ON SELMA

EASY FOR YOU TO SAY

Texas Agriculture Commissioner Reagan Brown, in a speech to agriculture professors from several western states, referred to Booker T. Washington as "the great black nigger—uh—educator—uh—excuse me for making that—the great black educator—the Negro educator."

THE COMBINATION PLATE

Judge Charles Stevens, who was appointed to the Santa Barbara County superior court by then-Governor Ronald Reagan, was censured by the California Supreme Court for racist remarks, including a reference to Hispanic Americans as "cute little tamales and Taco Bells."

WHAT'S BLACK AND BLUE...?

Claiming he'd instructed his staff to investigate why so many blacks die from police use of the carotid chokehold, L.A. police chief Daryl Gates said: "We may be finding that in some blacks when [the hold] is applied, the veins or arteries do not open up like...in normal people."

*

THANKS OF A GRATEFUL NATION

1981 Betsy Bloomingdale, a good friend of Nancy Reagan's, reported that one way she saved energy was "by asking my servants not to turn on the self-cleaning oven until after seven in the evening."

*

You Know Her, the Famous Reactress

1979 Dr. Edward Teller, father of the hydrogen bomb, took out a two-page ad in *The Wall Street Journal* to say that he was the only person whose health was affected by the Three Mile Island emergency: "I was [in Washington] to refute some of the propaganda that Ralph Nader, Jane Fonda and their kind are spewing to the news media.... I am 71 years old, and I was working 20 hours a day.... I suffered a heart attack.... I was the only one affected by the reactor.... No, that would be wrong. It was not the reactor. It was Jane Fonda."

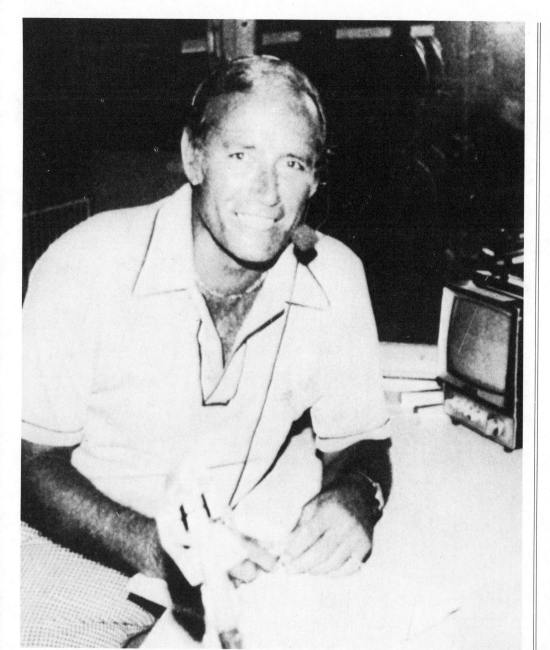

NEW!
FROM CHEF BOY-AR-DEE!

1969 Mrs. Elmer N. Bongean Jr. of Kaukana, Wisconsin, wrote a letter to the editor of *The Washington Post* in praise of Vince Lombardi. Lombardi, Mrs. Bongean said, would do wonders for America as coach of the nation's capital's team. "Peel away [Lombardi's] hard shell," she added, "and you have marshmallow simmering in Italian sauce."

∗

SAD BUT TRUE

1975 Los Angeles Police Chief Edward Davis said that women's liberation has brought America to the verge of "a crime wave like the world has never seen before," because today's amoral mothers are breeding a generation of savages. Crime would continue to rise, the chief added, because of the breakdown in traditional motherhood and "the new morality which condones lying, stealing and killing...a philosophic concept that has penetrated everyone who has gone to a university."

∗

Fear Grounds into a Double Play

1981 Chicago White Sox announcer Jimmy Piersall said that baseball wives are "horny broads that wanted to get married and get a little security and money." He also said that Greg Luzinski "should be shot" for not hustling on the field.

Daddy Dearest

1980 Nobel physicist and genetic theorist William Shockley told an interviewer that his own three children "represent a very significant regression" and attributed their shortcomings to their mother, who "had not as high an academic achievement standing as I."

80

SIS BOOM BAH

1971 Mrs. Patricia Bozell, sister of William and James Buckley and mother of ten, tried to punch out Ti-Grace Atkinson, a militant feminist, during a talk at Washington's Catholic University. Reason: Miss Atkinson reportedly had said, "The Blessed Virgin was knocked up."

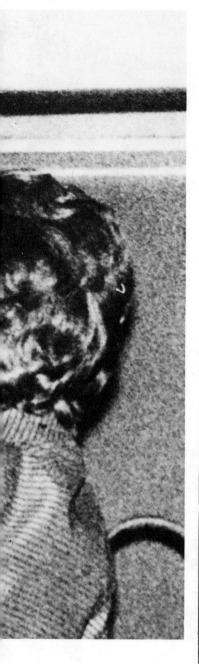

Down, Boy!

1977 On the scene at the Gary Gilmore execution, Geraldo Rivera frantically told ABC, "Kill the Rona segment. Get rid of it. You'll be able to hear the shots. I promise. You'll be able to hear the shots."

It Never Stopped Alfonse D'Amato

1981 Deborah Ann Fountain, twenty-five, this year's Miss New York State, was disqualified from the Miss U.S.A. pageant for stuffing her swimsuit. Claiming she'd lost weight, Fountain said: "I went from a 36 bust to a 34 bust. The suit was too big....I couldn't go onstage and represent New York State like that."

DIRTY COMMIE TRICK

1982 Svetlana Savitskaya of the Soviet Union became the second woman to be sent into space. When her spacecraft docked at an orbital space station, she was welcomed aboard by flight engineer Valentin Lebedev, who said, "We've got an apron ready for you, Sveta."

Great Ideas of Western Man: Part I

1976 Explaining his sexual philosophy in *Playboy*, Jimmy Carter said, "I've looked on a lot of women with lust. I've committed adultery in my heart many times…"

Great Ideas of Western Man: Part II

"…but that doesn't mean that I condemn someone who not only looks on a woman with lust but who leaves his wife and shacks up with somebody out of wedlock. Christ says don't consider yourself better than someone else because one guy screws a whole bunch of women while the other guy is loyal to his wife."

84

Special-Citation-Dubious-Achievement-Award-Good-for-a-Lifetime to George Romney

1967 Two years after a trip to Southeast Asia, Governor Romney announced, "I just had the greatest brainwashing that anyone can get when you go over to Vietnam, not only by the generals, but also by the diplomatic corps over there, and they do a very thorough job."

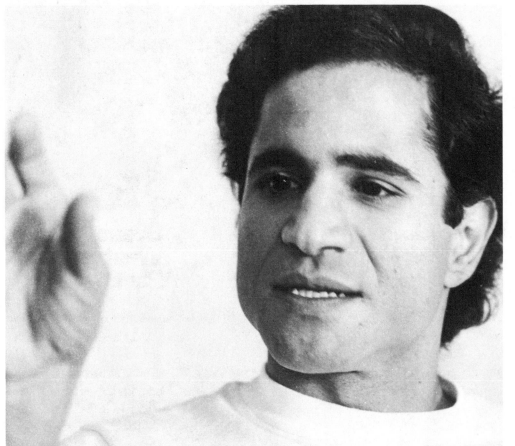

Sore Loser of 1982
Pleading for parole from Soledad prison in California, Sirhan Sirhan said: "If Robert Kennedy were alive today, he would not countenance singling me out for this kind of treatment."

KOJAK SPEAK

1975 Telly Savalas said that in his new movie he would expose "the greatest villain that ever lived, a man worse than Hitler or Stalin. I am speaking of Sigmund Freud."

GAG ME, LIKE, WITH A, YOU KNOW, SPOON

1982 David Crystal, a linguistics professor at Britain's Reading University, claimed that because tight, economical English isn't natural, speakers are better understood if they throw in a "ya know," an "I mean," or a "like" here and there. For instance, one can emphasize a point by changing the phrase "John and his friend" to "John and, you know, his friend."

✱

OH EARL, YOU BUTZ!

1976 Agriculture Secretary Earl Butz resigned after John Dean revealed that he overheard Butz telling Pat Boone that the only three things blacks want are, "first, a tight pussy; second, loose shoes; and, third, a warm place to shit."

✱

HOLIEST COW OF 1978

Sportscaster Phil Rizzuto, still on the air when told of Pope Paul VI's death, said, "Well, that kind of puts the damper on even a Yankee win."

✱

PRESIDENTIAL PRIVILEGE

1976 Moments before beginning an interview with David Frost, President Nixon turned to Frost and asked, "Well, did you do any fornicating this weekend?"

✱

WATCHING ALL THE GIRLS, WATCHING ALL THE GIRLS, WATCHING ALL THE GIRLS GROW BY

Miss America 1980, Cheryl Prewitt of Ackerman, Mississippi, pledged to donate 10 percent of her earnings in that year to church charities, since God was "the instigator of this whole thing." Describing a prayer meeting that took place years after a car accident that had left one of her legs shorter than the other, Prewitt said, "I sat and watched my leg grow out instantaneously two inches."

GIVE OR TAKE A COUPLE OF INCHES

Dr. George Miller of Northern Illinois University used a mathematical formula based on past pageant records to predict that Cheryl Prewitt would become Miss America 1980. The study concluded that the winner would most likely be from nineteen to twenty-three years old; would be at least a college junior but not a graduate student; would have a plain name; would live in a small town but not in Delaware, Maryland, Nebraska, Nevada, New Mexico, North Dakota, or Vermont; would rank highly in the swimsuit competition; would weigh between 105 and 135 pounds; and would stand between five feet four inches and five feet ten inches tall.

The 1979 Jean Hersholt Humanitarian Award to:

Producer Allan Carr, who said of *The Deer Hunter:* "I knew I wouldn't like it. It's about two things I don't care about: Vietnam and poor people."

NAME THE SECRETARY OF AGRICULTURE! QUICK!

1981 The Department of Agriculture proposed plans to save money on its school-lunch program by classifying sunflower seeds as "meat" and ketchup and pickle relish as "vegetables."

*

OKAY, ANNE FRANK, YOU CAN COME OUT NOW!

1975 Composer Richard Wagner's seventy-eight-year-old daughter-in-law, Winifred Wagner, who was a close friend of Adolf Hitler's for twenty-two years, told the world that der Führer had been misunderstood. He had a "good and human" nature, she said, "immensely appealing" eyes, and was "really touching with the children."

*

BUT A TRIP TO THE MOON ON GOSSAMER WINGS IT AIN'T

1976 The Beatrice, Nebraska, public-works department discovered that its newly installed $12,000 high-pressure sewer-cleaning system could force water in some toilets to shoot as high as the bathroom ceiling. A spokesman explained, "It's just one of those things."

*

SO GO

1980 *Soldier of Fortune* magazine held a three-day "celebration of war" in Columbia, Missouri. The seven hundred participants passed their time shooting guns, watching war movies, and getting drunk. Said one reveler, "I just want to go to Afghanistan and grease a few Ivans."

*

HRIGHT ON!

1970 Senator Roman Hruska (R-Neb.) defended President Nixon's nomination of G. Harrold Carswell to the Supreme Court, saying, "Even if he were mediocre, there are a lot of mediocre judges and people and lawyers, and they are entitled to a little representation, aren't they?"

But the Third Walks the Streets, a Free Lawyer

1976 Radical lawyer William Kunstler told a Dallas audience, "I'm not entirely upset by the Kennedy assassinations. In many ways, two of the most dangerous men in the country were eliminated."

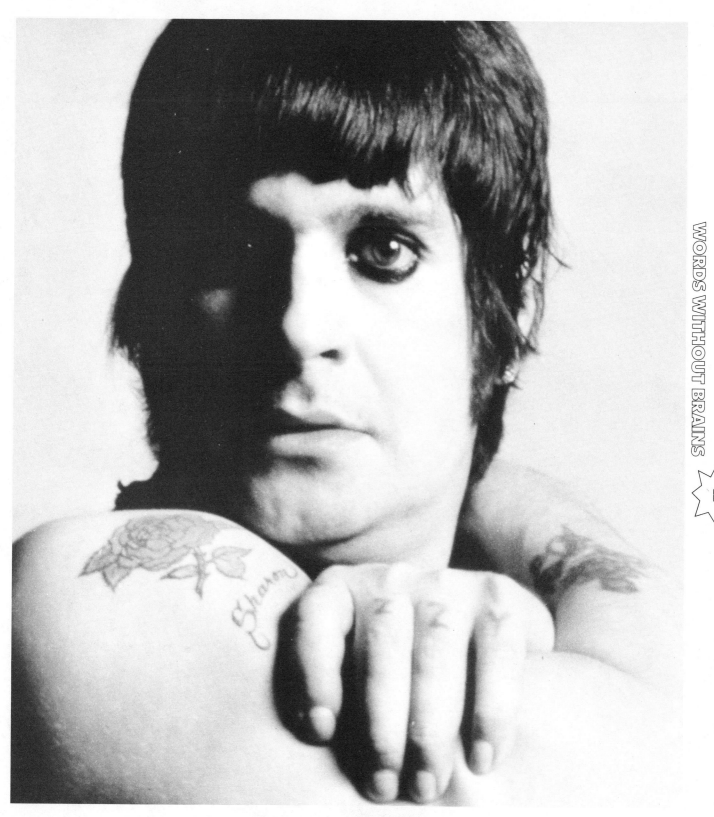

Remember Who?

1981 Rock star Ozzy Osbourne walked into a CBS records marketing meeting, pulled out a dead dove, and bit its head off. "I wanted them to remember me," he said.

TOUGH ACTS TO FOLLOW

A REAL FLIPPER TAPPER

1979 Graduate student Mark Gottlieb played the "aqualin" in a Stanford pool while his sister Karen accompanied him on the "hydrorgan."

✳

THEN HOW ABOUT OSCAR DE LA RUBBERS?

1982 The manufacturers of Sergio Valente jeans took legal action against a Philadelphia man who tried to market a prophylactic under the name Sergio Prevente.

✳

SEE STRIPE PLAY DEAD

1980 Highway workers in East Greenwich, Rhode Island, painted a yellow line across the body of a dead dog lying in their path.

✳

UNCLE HESHIE WENT OFF AT 6 TO 5

1980 Several employees at Sunrise Hospital in Las Vegas, Nevada, were suspended when it was discovered that they had made bets on how long critically ill patients would live. Investigators said the employees may even have acted to hasten the deaths of certain patients in order to protect their wagers.

✳

SEVEN YEARS OF VERMIN, LICE, AND LOCUSTS TO:

James Watt, Secretary of the Interior

Beef Jerky

1982 Interior Secretary James Watt redesigned his department's buffalo seal so that the animal faces right instead of left.

They've Got No Place to Go But Down

1983 Trapeze artists Arturo Goana and Naomi Rosas were married sixty feet above the crowd during a performance of the Shrine Circus in Houston.

The 1965 Watermelon Award to:

Robert Lloyd (a follower of George Lincoln Rockwell), who burst onto the floor of the House in blackface makeup, crying: "I's de Mississippi delegation!"

Why Can't He Abuse Himself in the Normal Way?

1975 Eleven-year-old Mark Harman of London, England, learned to do his homework while lying on a bed of four hundred nails with his six-year-old sister sitting on top of him.

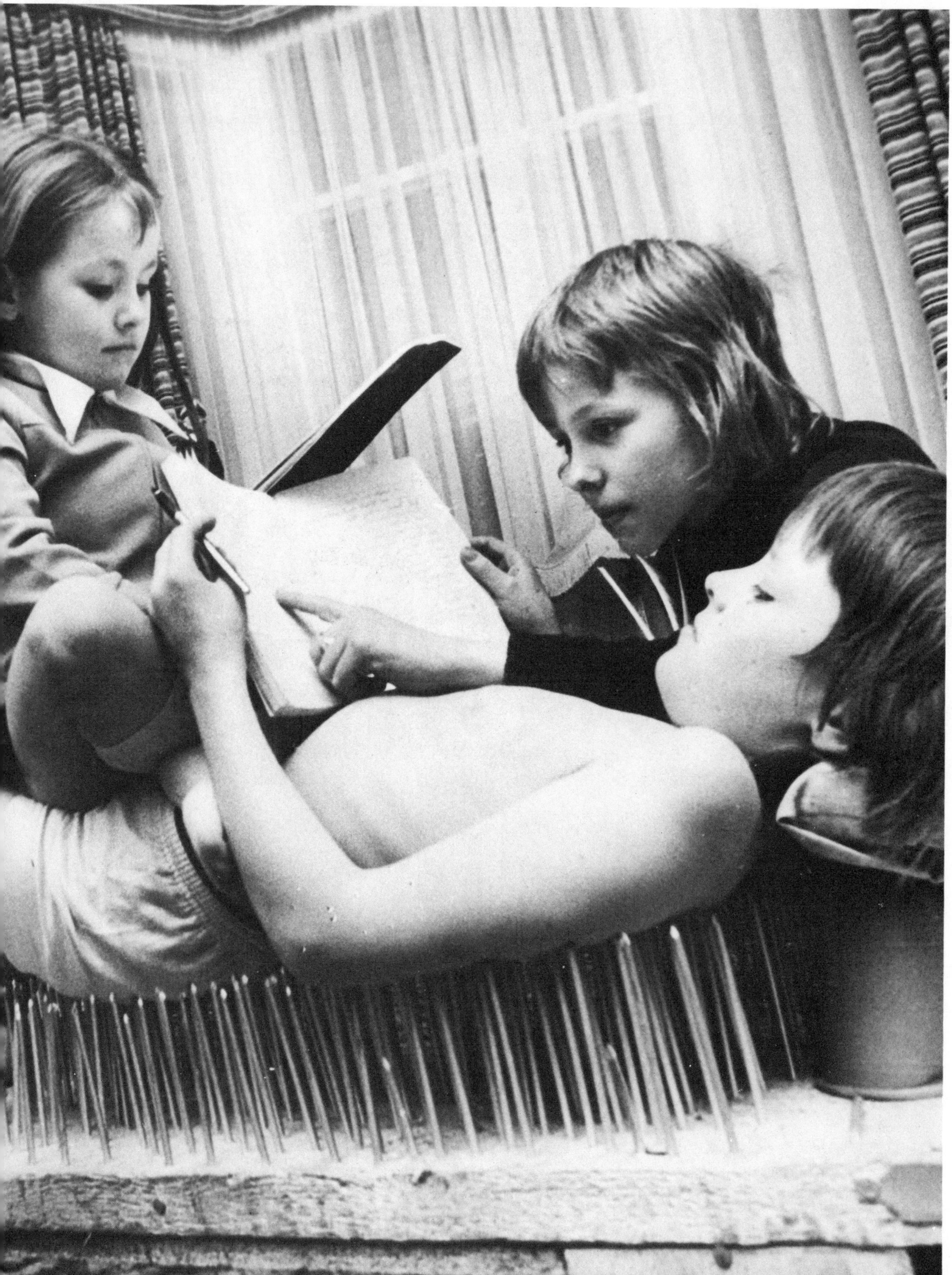

Worst Movies of the Year

1964: THE HORROR OF
PARTY BEACH

1963: CLEOPATRA

1965: THE SANDPIPER

1966: THE BIBLE

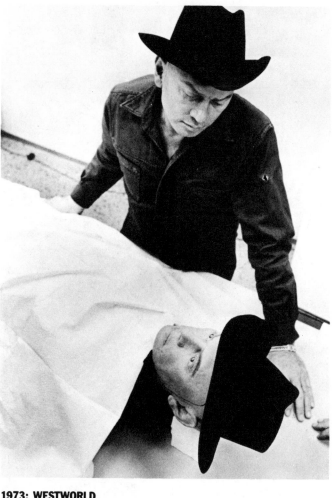

1973: WESTWORLD

1978: RABBIT TEST

1979: MOMENT BY MOMENT

1980: THE BLUE LAGOON

1981: TARZAN, THE APE MAN

1982: INCHON

Don't Tell Us, Tell Masters & Johnson
1983 Promoters tried to inflate a King Kong balloon, which lay slumped atop the Empire State Building for nearly a week.

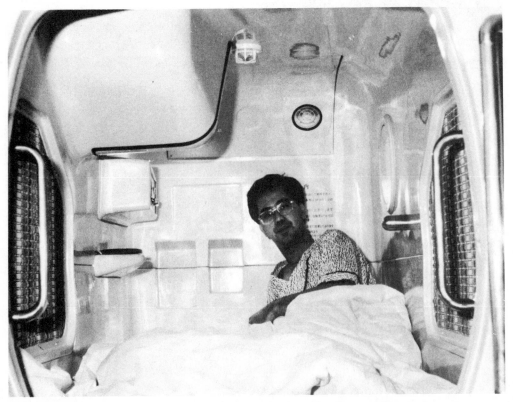

THEY CHECK IN, BUT THEY DON'T CHECK OUT
1981 The New Rubia, a 376-capsule hotel, opened in Osaka, Japan. For about $15 a night, a guest could stay in a sleeping capsule four feet eleven inches wide, six feet seven inches deep, complete with air conditioning and a color TV.

RARE PHOTO OF GERALD FORD'S CUSTOM-BUILT BULLETPROOF LIMOUSINE

RAINIEST DAYS OF THE YEAR

1966 February 10; 11 inches; Leesville, Louisiana

1967 September 22; 15.69 inches; Whitsett, Texas

1971 January 9; 12.38 inches; Pahoa, Hawaii

1973 June 14; 13.5 inches; Coldspring, Texas

1975 January 8; 15.9 inches; Hilo, Hawaii

1978 August 4; 29.05 inches; Albany, Texas

1979 July 26; 25 inches; Houston, Texas

1981 October 12; 22 inches; Breckenridge, Texas

*

THUS BREAKING THE OLD MARK SET BY HENRY KISSINGER IN '72
1976 Bob Fleming of Taylorville, Illinois, set a world record in the Illinois Cow Chip Championships by hurling a lump of cow manure 177.9 feet.

*

WE ESPECIALLY LIKED THE PEE DE DEUX

1980 The Toronto *Globe and Mail* reviewed a new dance program that featured a dancer who skipped to center stage carrying a pail, then sat down and urinated into it. The *Globe and Mail* described the program as a "ho-hum evening" of dance.

✳

IT DOESN'T BREATHE, IT GASPS

1980 John Coleman of Paw Paw, Michigan, developed Bermuda Beaujolais: wine made from onions.

✳

ELDRIDGE, YOU MADE THE APPURTENANCE TOO LONG

1975 Former Black Panther leader Eldridge Cleaver staged a one-man fashion show in Paris to introduce "Cleavers," high-waisted, bell-bottom men's pants with a kind of tube at the crotch. Discussing the advantages of what he calls "the appurtenance," Cleaver said, "There are some beautiful materials out for women's pants but men can't wear those. They can in my designs, since there is no mistaking they are men's pants."

✳

YEAH, BUT WAIT TILL YOU SEE "THE FLIGHT OF THE BUMBLEBEE"!

1967 The first topless quartet and topless conductor arrived from France and performed a series of private concerts across the U.S. First-violinist Michèle André said: "I can bow more freely and feel closer to Bach, my favorite, when I play partially undressed."

✳

SKYLAB MISSES SON OF SAM!

JULY 5

JULY 10

JULY 13

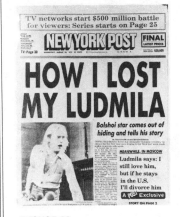

AUGUST 29

SEPTEMBER 12

SEPTEMBER 15

A contemplative retrospective on the year 1979—via the front pages of the *New York Post* (Rupert Murdoch, publisher, editor in chief, and Killer Bee *Numero Uno*):

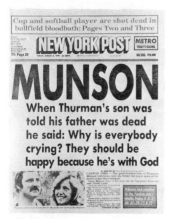

AUGUST 3

AUGUST 15

AUGUST 22

SEPTEMBER 17

SEPTEMBER 20

SEPTEMBER 21

I THINK THAT I SHALL NEVER SEE A TREE AS LOVELY AS AUNT BEA

1973 British doctor S. L. Henderson Smith urged that people stop burying or cremating their relatives and instead have the bodies ground up with sewage to be recycled as fertilizer.

*

IT'S NOT NICE TO FOOL MOTHER NATURE

1972 The Navy abandoned its highly secret Project Aquadog because it was unable to train dogs to swim underwater to kill enemy frogmen.

*

LOOKS LIKE A CASE FOR AQUADOG

1972 The women of Sipche, Nepal, poisoned all the men in their village because they believed that if they killed one hundred men, the hundredth would turn into gold and make them all rich.

*

Sore Losers of 1964

Yogi Berra got so rattled at shortstop Phil Linz on a bad day that he threatened to take Linz's harmonica away from him.

Fidel Castro, who was pitching for his side, decreed that since his team was still behind at the end of the ninth, the game would go into extra innings.

COME ON OUT, SPINKS, WE KNOW YOU'RE IN THERE

1981 A set of George Washington's false teeth was stolen from the National Museum of American History in Washington, D.C.

∗

MMMM...*RATATOUILLE!*

1980 Nelson Chaves, a Brazilian nutrition expert, urged his government to solve the nation's chronic food shortages by encouraging poor people to eat rats.

∗

TROUBLE IS, YOU HAVE TO PUT YOURSELF IN A BAGGIE AND SLEEP IN THE REFRIGERATOR

1980 Laboratoire Bio-Chimique of Canada manufactured pills that it said would enable users to tan without exposure to the sun. The U.S. Food and Drug Administration said that the pills, called Orobronze, contained a chemical food-coloring agent widely used in the production of butter and cheese.

∗

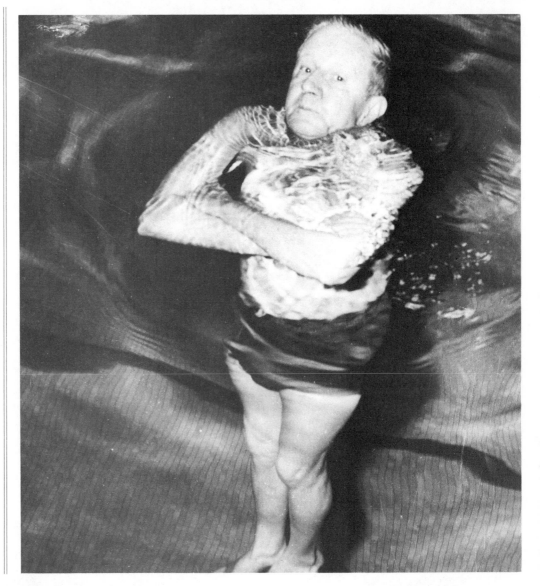

The New Leisure, Driver, and Step on It:

1964 Mr. Iver Johnson of Chicago, the "Human Cork," broke all records for floating in water vertically.

HI, I'M AQUADOG

Congratulations, Mr. Brown, You Have a Nine-Pound Souvenir of Atlantic City

1972 K. T. Maclay and Linda Sampson, New York designers, brought out a line of "pregnancy puffs," strap-on, oval-shaped pillows that make the wearer look pregnant.

JUST BE CAREFUL NOT TO ERASE IT

1977 The New-Clear Universal Foundation of Hollywood developed a program "to increase the size and thickness of the male organ" using only "a tape or cassette player and the hands."

✱

DIG HIS BODY, DIG HIS SOUL, LET'S ALL BOOGIE WITH THE PAPAL POLE!

1979 One of the year's bestselling records in Italy was a disco tune about Pope John Paul II that included the lyrics "He's the groove, he's the man/The new pope in the Vatican."

✱

NEXT THEY'LL BE SELLING TOE JAM IN THE GOURMET DEPARTMENT

1976 Bloomingdale's offered, for $450, beds in the shape of sneakers.

✱

IT'S 10 P.M. DO YOU KNOW WHERE YOUR KEN DOLL IS?

1978 Gay Bob, the world's first gay doll, came on the market, complete with flannel shirt, jeans, cowboy boots, and a closet he can come out of.

✱

A PLUCKY LITTLE RACE

1982 Shunici Muzuno, a Japanese robot designer, built a full-sized replica of Marilyn Monroe that smiles, breathes as its breasts gently heave, and sings a love song.

Thank You, Mr. President!

1965 Lyndon Johnson obligingly hoisted his shirt after his gall-bladder operation and showed us the scar—which we were all so eager to see.

FUN COUPLES

THE HONEYMOONIES

1982 The Reverend Sun Myung Moon married 2,075 couples, many of them strangers to each other, at Madison Square Garden.

✻

KINDA SAD HOW SOME COUPLES JUST SORTA DRIFT APART

1976 When Eugene Schneider's wife divorced him after thirty-three years of marriage, he cut their $80,000 New Jersey house in half with a chain saw.

Until the divorce case of sixty-four-year-old Sidney Watson and his sixty-six-year-old wife could be heard, a London judge devised a timetable to assure the feuding couple of privacy in the kitchen and the bathroom. Mr. Watson was given exclusive use of the living room and the back bedroom, while his wife was assigned the dining room and the front bedroom.

✻

IMPEACH EARL WARREN

1975 Las Vegas judge Keith Hayes divorced fifteen couples in six minutes by having them answer questions in unison. "It speeded up justice," said Hayes.

✻

1975 CHER AND GREGG ALLMAN

1975 BARBRA STREISAND AND JON PETERS

1982 ROBERT WAGNER AND JILL ST. JOHN

1980 CAMILLE HAGEN AND TATTOO

ATTENTION, BASKIN-ROBBINS!
1979 "We are so much alike," said Margaret Trudeau of her newfound companion, singer Lou Rawls (top). "Don't you think we could have a beautiful chocolate-colored daughter together?"

EXCEPT FOR THE CONVERTIBLE, WE

Two Hearts, Burning as One

1981 On April 11 Evangeline Gouletas of Chicago married Hugh Carey, governor of New York. Shortly before the wedding, Hugh Carey decided to dye his gray hair and eyebrows red. Shortly after the wedding, Evangeline Gouletas-Carey conceded an error in her marriage-license application, on which she'd claimed to have been married two previous times, not three. She said she thought that Frangiskos Kallaniotis, the overlooked ex-husband, was dead.

DON'T KNOW WHAT SHE SEES IN HIM

1981 PRINCE CHARLES AND
LADY DIANA

1980 MARY E. CUNNINGHAM AND WILLIAM M. AGEE

GEORGE STEINBRENNER AND BILLY MARTIN

1982 QUEEN ELIZABETH AND MICHAEL FAGAN

FIGURATIVELY, THAT MUST HAVE HURT A LOT

1979 Professor Marco Mason of New York admitted to biting off his wife's nose because she was "literally crushing" his testicles.

∗

POOR TONY WAS SECOND BEST

1973 When Tony Perkins married Berinthia Berenson on Cape Cod, Murray, his pet collie, was his best man.

∗

AT LEAST HE HAS A PLACE TO HANG OUT

1981 Paulo Cesar Bonfim walked halfway across Brazil carrying a large cross on his back to give thanks for his fiancée's recovery from a paralyzing disease. While he was gone, his fiancée married another man.

∗

GO ON, HAVE YOUR FUN. IT'S ALWAYS THE CHILDREN THAT SUFFER LATER

1976 Los Angeles secretary Jannene Swift married a fifty-pound pet rock in a formal ceremony in Lafayette Park.

∗

COMING UP NEXT: *HERPES HOTLINE*

1982 Mary Cooper, fifty-eight, and George Reese, sixty, both janitors, were married on the air after having met through a Cincinnati radio talk show called *Desperate and Dateless.*

∗

1979 MICHELLE TRIOLA AND LEE MARVIN

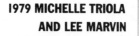

What Kind of Man Reads Soldier of Fortune?

1981 Donald Lee Laisure, a self-described millionaire, married convicted mass murderer Susan Atkins, a former member of the Charles Manson family.

...AND CONRAD HILTON JR., 1950

Liz A Many-Splendored Thing

THIS IS MY BELOVED
Richard Burton, who was married twice to Elizabeth Taylor, once told a reporter: "She has a double chin and an overdeveloped chest and she's rather short in the leg. So I can hardly describe her as the most beautiful creature I've ever seen."

...AND MICHAEL WILDING, 1952

...AND MIKE TODD, 1957

114

...AND EDDIE FISHER, 1959

...AND RICHARD BURTON, 1965

...AND JOHN WARNER, 1981

...AND VICTOR LUNA, 1983

WARREN

Would You Kick This Life Out of Bed?

TESTIMONIALS

Julie Christie on Warren Beatty: "He eats, well—like a baboon."

Joan Collins on Warren Beatty: "He was insatiable. Three, four, five times a day, every day, was not unusual for him, and he was also able to accept phone calls at the same time."

Britt Ekland on Warren Beatty: "Warren could handle women as smoothly as operating an elevator. He knew exactly where to locate the top button. One flick and we were on the way."

Faye Dunaway on Warren Beatty: "He's no fool, Warren."

...AND JOAN COLLINS, 1960

...AND NATALIE WOOD, 1962

...AND LESLIE CARON, 1964

...AND JULIE CHRISTIE, 1971

...AND MICHELLE PHILLIPS, 1975

...AND DIANE KEATON, 1982

DoublePlay

1973 Yankee pitcher Fritz Peterson (center) divorced his wife, Marilyn Peterson (left), to marry Susan Kekich (right), wife of teammate Mike Kekich, who in turn married the former Mrs. Peterson.

1982 MARTINA NAVRATILOVA AND NANCY LIEBERMAN

1981 RITA AND JOHN JENRETTE

1979 MEGAN MARSHACK AND NELSON ROCKEFELLER

I DON' KNOW, MARTY, WHADDA YOU WANTA DO TONIGHT?

1982 The marriage of Ernest Borgnine to Ethel Merman lasted exactly five weeks.

**1981 MARILYN BARNETT AND
BILLIE JEAN KING**

WHICH TWIN
HAS THE TONI?

WAC-Offs of the Year

1973 Gail Bates and Valerie Randolph were discharged from the Women's Army Corps after they confessed to being married homosexuals. The women charged that they turned gay because there was nothing else to do in the Army.

1982 ROXANNE AND PETER PULITZER

THERE BUT FOR THE GRACE OF GOD GOES OLA-FLORENCE NIXON

1970 At a White House reunion of the Whittier College Class of 1934, President Nixon failed to recognize Ola-Florence Welch, whom he dated off and on for six years and once advised, following an argument, "When I see you again, it'll be too soon."

Don't Do Anything Rash

1981 Ted and Joan Kennedy announced plans for a divorce.

A Sticky Legal Issue

1982 Lee Perry, a female Harvard University professor who'd sued Dr. Richard Atkinson, chancellor of the University of California at San Diego, because he refused to make her pregnant, said she would drop the suit in exchange for Dr. Atkinson's sperm.

Call Me Schlemiel

1982 Sammy Davis Jr. met with Prime Minister Menachem Begin on a visit to Israel, his "religious homeland." "When we shook hands," said Davis, "I felt a wave of heat go through my body, like electricity." Begin, in turn, called Davis "a genius."

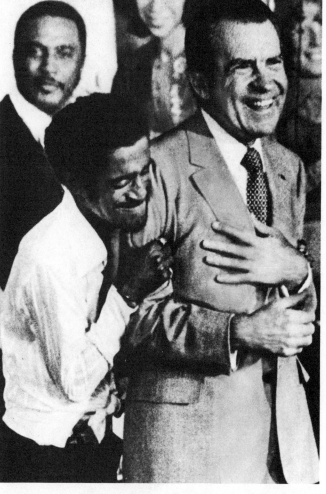

I WON'T DANCE, DON'T ASK ME

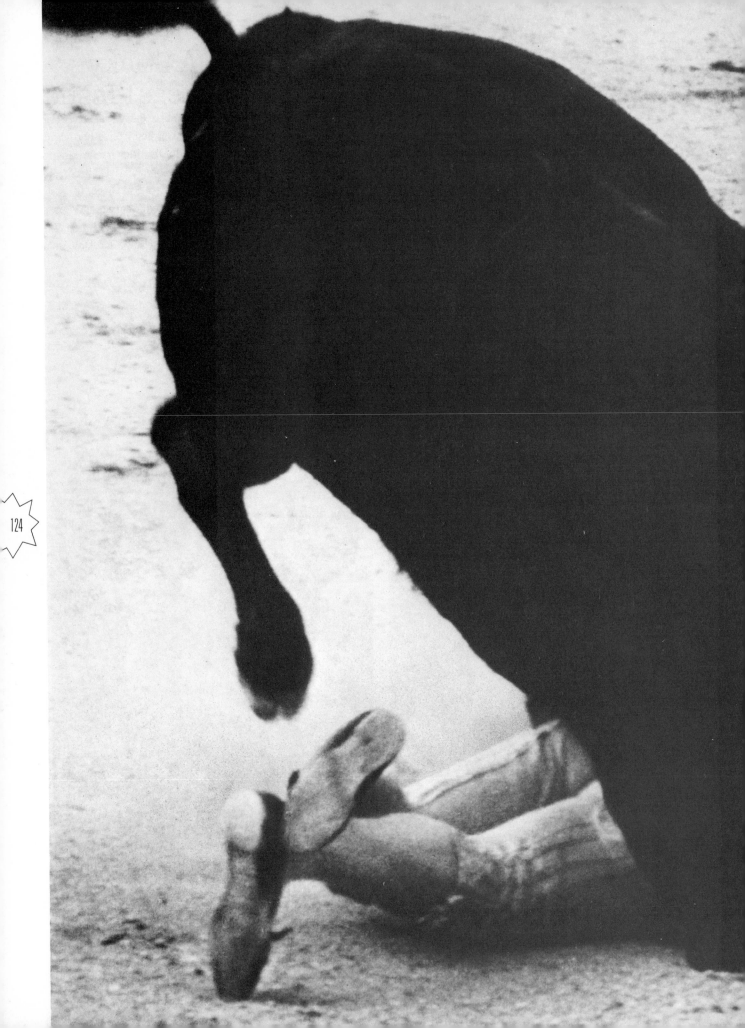

OOPS!

THE KLUTZ OF SUMMER
1966 Willie Davis of the Los Angeles Dodgers made three consecutive errors in one inning in a World Series game (two dropped balls, one wild throw).

WHICH HE CUT OFF AND GAVE TO HIS GIRL FRIEND

1983 During the ninth bullfight at the San Isidro Fair in Madrid, Ortiz, a banderillero for Mexican bullfighter Jorge Gutierrez, lay low to avoid a charging bull. He escaped with only minor scratches on his nose.

＊

THE WHITE GLOVES GAVE HER AWAY

1982 A medical student at the University of Alabama discovered to her shock that one of the cadavers her dissection class was to work on was in fact her great aunt.

＊

CAUTION—
SPEED BUMPS AHEAD

1982 Ireland set out to crack down on alcohol-related traffic accidents. A spokesman for the Automobile Association in Dublin said it's time to stop blaming accidents on motorists: "In many cases the pedestrian is to blame. Often, he is lying prone in the roadway."

＊

SAY, WHAT?

1976 ABC's audio system failed, causing a twenty-seven-minute silence during the first Ford-Carter Presidential debate.

＊

TUSHÉ!

Use the Rocks, Dummy!

1966 Six hundred spectators paid $20 to $100 apiece to watch L. S. Rao, "exponent of Yoga," walk on water. Rao warmed up by swallowing what he said were steel tacks and nitric acid, then skipped across hot embers. He then stepped onto the surface of the water and instantly sank to the bottom.

Après Moi, La Stupidité

1981 Gerald Ford told Valéry Giscard d'Estaing that he regretted never having visited France while he was President of the United States. In fact, Ford had attended a summit conference in that country in 1975.

IT WAS ALL THOSE LOBSTERS IN SUNGLASSES ON ROLLER SKATES

1978 German tourist Erwin Kreuz, en route from his native land to the West Coast, stepped off his plane at a fueling stop in Bangor, Maine, and spent four days there thinking he was in California.

∗

BOO, HISS!

1969 President Richard Nixon opened the baseball season by dropping the first ball.

∗

DO I HAVE TIME FOR THIS STORY?

1971 While taping a *Dick Cavett Show*, nutrition expert J. I. Rodale said, "I'm so healthy I expect to live on and on." He then dropped dead of a heart attack.

∗

DON'T BLAME DESENEX!

1982 Thirteen-year-old Doug Pritchard of Lenoir, North Carolina, found a painful lump on his left foot. The doctor he consulted discovered a tooth growing there.

∗

"OM."
"HONK!"
"OM."
"HONK!"
"OM!"
"HONK!"
THWACK!

1981 A Northern Illinois University student was charged with destruction of university property after he killed William, the campus goose. The student, who was sitting by a lagoon, whirled and struck the goose on the head with a stick when the bird startled him out of his "deep meditation."

∗

FAULT!

1979 Linda Siegel, an eighteen-year-old from Piedmont, California, fell out of her tennis dress during a Wimbledon match with Billie Jean King.

DOUBLE FAULT!

Betty Stewart, who lent Linda Siegel the dress she fell out of, played at Wimbledon in a set of knickers embroidered with the words WATCH IT.

I See London... I See France...

At Least He Didn't Ask Him to Shuck and Jive

1981 At a White House reception for the nation's mayors, President Reagan went up to a black man and shook his hand and said, "How are you, Mr. Mayor? I'm glad to meet you. How are things in your city?" The man, Samuel Pierce, was Reagan's Secretary of Housing and Urban Development.

DON'T RAISE THE BRIDGE, PUT OUT THE RIVER

1969 Cleveland's Cuyahoga River, running through the industrial center, caught fire because of an excess of pollution.

Darn!

1971 Captain Eugene Kotouc was acquitted by a military judge after testifying he'd accidentally cut off a Vietnamese prisoner's fingertip while seeking vital information.

OR JUST ENOUGH FOR A LONG WEEKEND IN THE HAMPTONS

1980 Mary Bates sued a Homer, Michigan, funeral parlor after her deceased husband fell through the bottom of his casket as he was being carried to his grave. The suit claimed that the shoddy coffin contained, in addition to Mr. Bates, "rags, newspapers, shredded paper, and pantyhose."

✴

FROM THE HALLS OF MONTEZUMA TO THE SHORES OF WHATSITSNAME

1975 The United States Marines, in attempting to rescue the crew of the *Mayaguez*, invaded the wrong Cambodian island.

✴

GARFIELD GOES BANANAS

1983 Dale Davis of Greenwood, Indiana, was shot in the finger by his cat while sitting in his living room. According to police, the cat and a .38-caliber pistol were on a nearby coffee table; when the cat jumped, the gun went off.

✴

OKAY, OKAY, WHO MOVED THE BRIDGE?

1969 Work came to a halt on a bridge and highway in Pennsylvania when workmen found that they were going to miss each other by thirteen feet.

✴

CZECHMATE!

1972 Mrs. Vera Czermak of Prague, learning that her husband had betrayed her, attempted suicide by jumping out a third-story window. She landed on her husband, killing him.

✴

132

Hello, Hello, Dolly

1978 Just before accepting the Entertainer of the Year award from the Country Music Association, Dolly Parton burst the front of the dress she had made for her for the occasion.

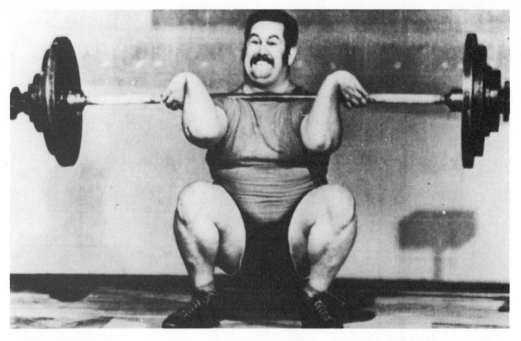

LISTEN, KID, YOU'RE GOING OUT

THERE A BIG CLUMSY ANIMAL BUT

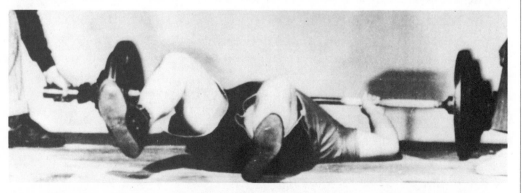

YOU'RE COMING BACK A STAR

LET 'EM EAT STAPLES
1981 *The Bangkok Post* reported that cashews being sold for higher prices as "whole" had actually been glued together.

*

IT'S 10 P.M.
DO YOU KNOW WHERE
YOUR GUPPIES ARE?
1976 Four Florida pet shops mistakenly sold to Tampa fish collectors twenty-three piranhas.

*

LET'S RING THEIR
LITTLE COLLARS!
1980 When third-grade students in a Connecticut grammar school were asked to spell the word *relief*, more than half of them answered, "R-O-L-A-I-D-S."

*

OOH, GRODY TO THE MAX!
1982 Stephen Midgley, the manager of a McDonald's in London, was fired after a customer was served french fries with cigarette butts; a mustard, cola, and pickle juice milkshake; and fish sprinkled with pencil sharpenings.

*

AS GREAT AS GEORGE
WASHINGTON CARVER?
1980 Accepting his renomination for President, Jimmy Carter paid tribute to "a great man who should have been President and would have been one of the greatest Presidents in history—Hubert Horatio Hornblower."

*

WHY?
WAS THERE A HOLE IN IT?
1981 A jury in Newport, Tennessee, ordered Stokely-Van Camp's Inc. to pay a man $2,500 after he found a condom in a can of the company's pork and beans.

*

CREDITS

*   *   *   *   *   *   *

Without the assistance of United Press International, several dubious achievements in this book might have been lost to history. The editors of *Esquire* would like to acknowledge this invaluable aid, with special thanks to Stan Friedman. All photographs reproduced in this book and on the front and back covers are from UPI, with the exception of those listed below.

Pages 2–3, 4: Ball of twine, *Minneapolis Star and Tribune.* **Page 5:** Bark mitzvah, Tony Jerome. **Page 6:** Stimorol, David Hamsley. **Page 7:** Van Halen, Courtesy of Warner Bros. Records. **Page 8:** Underwear, Courtesy of David Lloyd. **Page 12:** Wide World Photos. **Page 14:** Ronald Reagan, Sygma. **Pages 16–17:** Beer-can shroud, Janice Rubin. **Page 18:** David Chabira and John Benaka, and Mark Pauga, Sterling Publishing Co. **Page 20:** R. J. Galbraith. **Page 21:** Statue of Sylvester Stallone, Mort Bond; Stanford Cohen, Wide World Photos. **Page 22:** Carolyn Farb, Shelly Katz/Black Star. **Page 27:** Dennis Rainear, Wide World Photos. **Pages 32–33, 34:** Pia Zadora, Wide World Photos. **Page 37:** Maddox in oversize glasses, Wide World Photos. **Page 40:** Amintore Fanfani and Angelo Gallo, Wide World Photos. **Page 41:** Pierre Trudeau, and Bella Abzug, Wide World Photos. **Page 44:** Hubert Humphrey, Wide World Photos. **Page 45:** Jimmy Carter, Wide World Photos. **Page 47:** Movie Star News. **Page 48:** Sygma. **Page 49:** *Mona Lisa* portrait, Courtesy of the Ambassade de France. **Page 50:** Wide World Photos. **Page 53:** Wide World Photos. **Page 54:** Anita Ekberg, Photo Trends. **Page 55:** Gerald Ford (photos nos. 2 and 3 in series), Wide World Photos. **Page 56:** Wide World Photos. **Page 57:** Twiggy, Wide World Photos. **Page 58:** Barbra Streisand, Movie Star News. **Page 62:** Ingemar Johansson, Wide World Photos; chopped-liver Brooke Shields, Anne Fishbein. **Page 67:** Frog, Wide World Photos. **Page 68:** 21st-century woman, and Koko, Wide World Photos. **Page 71:** Wide World Photos. **Pages 74–75, 76:** Martha Mitchell, Wide World Photos. **Page 76:** Frank Rizzo, Wide World Photos. **Page 77:** Grace Slick's baby, Wide World Photos. **Page 84:** Sirhan Sirhan, Peter Tatiner/Gamma-Liaison. **Page 89:** Ozzy Osbourne, Courtesy of CBS Records. **Page 93:** Buffalo seal, D. Gorton/*New York Times* Pictures. **Pages 96–97:** *The Horror of Party Beach, Westworld, Moment by Moment, Rabbit Test,* and *Inchon,* Movie Star News; *Tarzan* and *The Blue Lagoon,* Wide World Photos. **Pages 100–101:** *New York Post* covers, Preston Lyon. **Page 102:** Iver Johnson, and Aqua Dog, Wide World Photos. **Page 104:** Marilyn Doll, Wide World Photos. **Pages 106–107, 108:** The Moonies, Gamma-Liaison. **Page 109:** Robert Wagner and Jill St. John, Alan Berliner/Gamma-Liaison. **Page 110:** Hugh Carey and bride, FPG. **Page 114:** Elizabeth Taylor in headdress, Armando Pietrangeli/Globe Photos; Elizabeth Taylor and Richard Burton, Tom Wargacki/Globe Photos. **Page 118:** Megan Marshack, Wide World Photos. **Page 120:** Theodore White, Carl Mydans/Black Star; Yoda, Movie Star News; Marilyn Barnett and Billie Jean King, Curt Gunther/Camera Five. **Page 123:** Sammy Davis Jr. and Richard Nixon, and Lee Perry, Wide World Photos. **Page 130:** Cuyahoga River, Mitchael Zaremba. **Page 133:** Wide World Photos. **Back Cover:** The Moonies, Gamma-Liaison; Twiggy, Wide World Photos; Teeth, *New York Times* Pictures; pig, Neil Selkirk; Martha Mitchell, Wide World Photos.

Design assistance by John Orth and Charles Brucaliere.

**IF WE'VE ASKED YOU
ONCE, WE'VE ASKED YOU A
THOUSAND TIMES:**

Why Is This Man Laughing?